PRAISE FOR

"We've watched Jeff grow from paperboy to his first paperback, and this book illustrates how he has learned to tackle challenges with a caring people-first approach. We're proud of our son!"

—Mom and Dad Skipper

"I've had the pleasure of working with Jeff on several projects and he does what he says. You will find practical help in this book!"

—Jennifer McCue, President & CEO, Bethany Care Society

"The world is not going to get any calmer any time soon, but Jeff creates great clarity in the eye of the storm and teaches us all how to tame the winds in our favor."

—Alan Weiss, PhD., author of Sentient Strategy, Million Dollar Consulting, and over 60 other books

Change has become a dirty word, but it doesn't need to be. Dancing with Disruption equips leaders with strategies to overcome or even welcome change—because without change there is no growth.

—Laurie Wang, Vice President, People, Culture and Communications, Legal Aid Alberta

"Having worked directly with Jeff, I can say that he knows exactly what he's talking about. He has helped my organization successfully lead a massive amount of change by shifting mindset and behavior."

—Alyssa Better, Director, Global Sales Enablement, Quest

DANCING WITH DISRUPTION

LEADING DRAMATIC CHANGE DURING GLOBAL TRANSFORMATION

JEFF SKIPPER

Dancing with Disruption: Leading Dramatic Change During Global Transformation

Published by Peacebridge Publishing

ISBN: 978-1-7389038-0-1
BUSINESS & ECONOMICS / Management

Cover and interior design by Victoria Wolf, wolf designandmarketing,com. Copyright owned by Jeff Skipper.

No author stands alone. To my family, thank you for letting me run away to write in far-off places.

CONTENTS

ACKNOWLEDGMENTS

To Alan Weiss, the rockstar of consulting. This book would not exist without your encouragement. To Steven Bleistein, for an awesome title!

INTRODUCTION: AN UNPARALLELED LESSON IN HOW TO LEAD CHANGE

AS A LEADER YOU ARE RESPONSIBLE to make change happen when needed. Quickly. You have to adapt to shifts in customer behavior, labor shortfalls, and competitor attacks. You have a workforce that needs to keep pace.

- How do you motivate people to change fast? Even overnight?
- How do you sell that goal — and the change process required to get there?
- How do you filter out rumors and untruths when rolling out dramatic change?
- How do you know when to reward change? Or coerce it?
- How do you get hundreds or thousands of people aligned on a single goal?

In early 2020, everyone experienced an event that demanded rapid, radical change. As the COVID-19 pandemic spread relentlessly through our cities and nations, government and health leaders asked us to change fundamental behaviors overnight. No touching. Keep six feet apart. Don't visit your neighbor or your grandkids. Cancel your plans. Start sanitizing as if your life depends on it.

As the crisis unfolded, governments took action. Many different actions. Some were outrageous. Some were contradictory. All were focused on driving change in people's behavior. Some governments, like New Zealand, succeeded in their approach to curtail the virus with draconian rules. In nations slower to adopt measures, major surges killed thousands.

The way we shopped, ate, and socialized became fundamentally different. Parents became teachers, teachers became online influencers, and managers became mental health consultants.

Some of these changes were transient, and reversion was quick. (Back to the gym for me!) Others have become permanent, baked in by a blend of positive experiences (food delivered to my door!) and fear (long COVID is horrible).

Organizations proved they could transform faster than ever imagined. Long-term projects to carry out digital transformation and enable remote work suddenly had extremely short timelines — and they got done.

It was the largest experiment ever witnessed in promoting behavior change on a scale never seen before or in such a short timeframe, offering an unparalleled lesson in how to lead dramatic change. From money to mandates, leaders used every tool available to inspire and coerce compliance to behave in a new way. The pandemic gave us all a perfect view of how change can — and cannot — be led.

What made the difference between success and failure in this change effort? What could have been improved? If we pause to review the choices and results, there is much to learn. This book is your guide to drive dramatic change in your organization. It uses the pandemic as a case study for the application of change leadership.

Note the choice of term. Change management is a follower's game. Someone else is pushing the buttons, and you are simply responding. When it comes to rapid transformation, strong leadership is essential, and the focus must be on the end goal and the change required to reach that goal. Change leadership is the focal point of our work in driving success.

We will dive into twelve strategies used during the pandemic to unlock truths about leading change — our dance in the face of disruption — to help you repeat what works and avoid wasting time on what doesn't. I will assess why leaders' strategies were or were not effective using the principles of psychology coupled with my own experience of leading change across every type of industry and with every type of stakeholder for more than twenty-five years.

Briefly, the twelve change leadership strategies we will investigate are:

1. Set a clear goal
2. Identify all stakeholders
3. Assess impacts
4. Develop a change plan

5. Lead the change
6. Execute the plan
7. Communicate effectively
8. Remove barriers
9. Respond to resistance
10. Measure success
11. Sustain success
12. Clean up

Never has the discipline of leading change been more relevant, visible, and widespread. The advice in this book will guide you to successfully lead any type of significant change effort. Keep in mind that — while I analyze the challenges, successes, and failures of change leadership related to the pandemic — my goal is to offer insights and proven strategies for you as a business leader so you can successfully implement dramatic change in your organization.

Here are just a few takeaways you'll learn:

- To inspire broad change, you need a clear destination as well as consequences for failure.
- Change does not apply to everyone in the same way. Inspiration is a one-to-one game.
- You can predict resistance in two minutes with two simple questions, which we'll discuss in Strategy 3.
- Strategies for change often fail on first use. Rapid response to changing realities on the front line enables success.
- Having multiple leaders erodes the effectiveness of change initiatives. You must choose a single leader carefully.

- The biggest issue in communicating change is getting above the noise.
- The biggest barrier to change is often barriers. Removing limitations related to time, travel, and language can be your biggest boost to adoption.
- You can't sustain change without rewarding people, but it's better to highlight benefits than hand out cash and gifts.
- You can coerce change, but you will pay the price in broader resistance among your converts.
- Measurements drive motivation. Monitor leading and lagging measurements to keep your change plan on track.

If you are leading employees through a major disruption, you will gain useful, practical insights here. Put on your mask, and let's take a closer look.

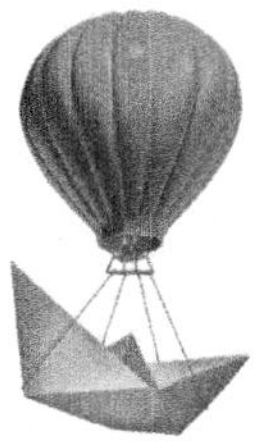

STRATEGY 1 START AT THE END: SET A CLEAR GOAL

"If you don't know where you're going,
every road will get you nowhere."

—Henry Kissinger

YOU CAN'T LEAD CHANGE WITHOUT a clear destination. We begin at the end. It's a simple point too often missed in the rush to demonstrate that action is happening. Think about the politicians who want to claim progress in the pursuit of popularity. Quick wins can lead to big losses if we are not moving in the right direction.

Clarity on the goal eliminates confusion, sets guidelines for tactics, and avoids wasted time and effort. But we can't pursue just any direction. The end goal needs to make sense and appeal to the people you are leading. With the onset of the COVID-19 pandemic in 2020, stakes were never higher. The goal for change had to inspire the entire world.

THE EVIDENCE

At first glance, the answer to "What is the goal?" seems obvious when it came to the pandemic. The 1918 influenza pandemic (commonly known as the Spanish flu) demonstrated just how deadly a virus can be. Twenty years ago, SARS was also instructive. When the COVID-19 pandemic struck, the direction from the World Health Organization was to preserve lives. Governments adopted a similar stance and put saving lives before all other priorities. As a top-level goal, that is pretty easy to support. Who wouldn't? There was no cure at the outset. The threat was real.

By summer 2020, with no vaccine available and infection numbers swelling, it would have been foolish to focus on a return to normal. Savings lives physically was extremely difficult. Hospitals were overloaded. Sickness, fear, and survival instincts made for many perspectives on what "saving lives" truly meant, such as:

- Eliminate the threat of dying from the virus at any cost
- Protect the vulnerable
- Enable people to keep working
- Save small businesses
- Save all businesses
- Prevent Amazon from taking over all retail
- Preserve freedom to do whatever the heck I want
- Let me visit my grandkids.
- Return life to the way things were ASAP!

These were all valid goals. But were they equal in importance? While the primary goal remained obvious — keep people alive

— secondary goals varied widely. Many governments stepped in to save businesses and protect individuals who could not go to work with loans and subsidies. They were saving livelihoods as well as lives.

Once vaccines became available, secondary goals shifted and split again. In the spirit of saving lives and moving toward loosening of restrictions, leaders altered the message: Everyone should be vaccinated. It's our best defense against death or the horrors of long COVID.

SET A CLEAR GOAL: THE ANALYSIS

In early 2020, COVID-19 infections spread at a frightening speed. Government and health leaders needed to respond quickly. Regarding our first strategy — set a clear goal — how well did they do?

I have assigned a score of A, B, C, or D for each of the twelve strategies you'll read about in this book. While my scores are admittedly subjective, my hope is that assigning each strategy a rating will give you added perspective on how well leaders applied the strategy during this change process. As a side benefit, perhaps this will inspire you to hold lively "water cooler conversations" with other change leaders to debate these scores!

So, let's return to our question. When it came to setting a clear goal, how well did leaders do?

Score: A

Setting the goal for a dramatic change is tricky business. It requires you to predict the future and envision where the change will lead. A virus with no cure made that problematic. When the end game is a blur, it's wise to pick a strong intermediate goal, which is what our leaders did. Saving lives was a logical immediate target.

The goal of saving lives was broad enough to incorporate a focus on saving livelihoods, creating vaccines, and defending against the surge of variants. Saving lives included keeping businesses afloat and helping individuals pay their bills when work was restricted. The goal was clear enough to give everyone direction and broad enough to encompass many different tactics to accomplish it. From a leadership perspective, that's extremely helpful, providing great latitude for innovation.

The goal for the pandemic was clearly related to people. I know it's obvious, but it's worth stating that when leaders cannot show a clear connection between disruption and how it will benefit individuals, it's much more difficult to move people to change. In the case of the pandemic, the disruptive change of safety measures would not only benefit each of us as individuals but it would also benefit our larger community. We chose to comply with restrictions for the collective safety of our friends, family, and neighbors as much as for ourselves.

Of course, not everyone was happy with the restrictions leaders put in place to accomplish the goal. Even with the right goal in mind, those measures would damage the economy in ways that might not be recoverable — at least not for a long time. And those restrictions would impact mental health. One must ask, "What is the life to be preserved?" Isolation and idleness are not "living." Sacrifices were necessary, which gave rise to protests, but national governments did not waver from their main goal of saving lives.

As vaccines became widely available, local governments adjusted their goals. While national governments continued to press for saving physical lives through vaccination, some local governments (for example, Texas and Alberta) began shifting priorities to saving the economy and preserving the rights of individuals to choose how they would live. (For many, "choice" centered on whether to wear a mask or get vaccinated.) While this was a significant change in focus, it still fell within the broader umbrella of the main goal. The burden of change moved from the majority to those who were the most vulnerable, making vaccination a matter of choice rather than a mandate and leaving those at risk to adjust habits to ensure their own safety.

COVID-19 has taken millions of lives worldwide. For the few countries that chose a hands-off approach with no goal to save lives, they did not achieve herd immunity nor inspire behaviors that would prevent the spread. Instead, they witnessed major surges in infections and a large number of deaths.

Governments that set a goal to put lives above all else made the goal clear from the beginning and were able to align the majority of their citizens with changes that helped to support the achievement of that goal.

LESSONS FOR CHANGE LEADERS

Different people have different priorities. We act in our own self-interest. To get everyone aligned and moving in the same direction one goal must rule them all. Change cannot be about 100 things. It must have a single, clear focus that encompasses varied interests while being resilient enough to withstand shifts in circumstances. Yes, it can encompass a few secondary priorities, as long as they clearly align with the main goal. If you can't illustrate the end goal with clarity because it is still being defined, pick an intermediate goal that will get your audience moving.

When announcing the goal for change, your audience needs a well-defined view of all that the goal entails: the who, what, why, when, and where.

- Where are we going?
- Who is impacted?
- What will I need to do differently?
- What's in it for me? Will it hurt?
- Why are we doing this?
- When will this happen?

You might have noticed that how is missing from this list. We will get to this when we begin working on tactics. When you roll out a new change, it's common to still be mapping out the how. Tell your audience that the details are coming and give them a timeline. It's still important to get them thinking about the goal while you are still working out the details.

Painting a detailed picture of the future that highlights the benefits of the change infuses it with purpose, making it easier for people to support. Your audience needs to know that the change process is worth it. Connecting the goal with benefits for each person is an important motivator. Connecting the goal with benefits for others can be even more powerful. Helping those around us offers purpose and meaning to our lives, a common desire for everyone.

We can't ignore the fact that nothing great or noble is accomplished without giving up something. Pursuing a goal means not pursuing something else. Sacrifice is inherent. It's the nature of change, and people recognize costs right away. Many changes in our organizations today such as system upgrades and departmental shuffles don't appear to have any direct benefits for employees. The change just needs to be done.

During the pandemic, couples delayed marriages, and families could not reunite. My wife and I watched the news closely, wondering if our planned anniversary trip to London and Paris would happen. As one by one the borders closed, we gave up hope for our special trip. Two years later, that milestone anniversary to be celebrated is long gone, and we can't get it back. Others gave up much more. It was all pain with no gain.

As leaders, we must be sensitive to the negative side of change and call it out early and often, both to prepare people for it and to acknowledge the pain. Help people shoulder the pain, if possible. At minimum, demonstrate empathy.

Laying out the goal clearly enables people to begin processing the reality of the change and the pain it may bring so they are prepared for what comes next.

TAKEAWAYS FOR YOUR CHANGE INITIATIVE

- Set a single overarching goal for the change. Make it as clear as possible.
- If the end vision is unclear at the moment, choose an interim goal that is clear.
- Keep the goal at a high enough level to allow for different approaches to achievement. Don't be specific on the how yet; focus on the who, what, why, when, and where.
- Ensure secondary goals are positioned as such, and make sure they align with the main goal.
- Make the goal purposeful — connect it to beneficial outcomes for people who are impacted (directly or indirectly), including the individual employees and their coworkers, customers, friends, family, and communities as well as shareholders and any other stakeholders.
- Increase motivation by connecting the change with benefits for others.

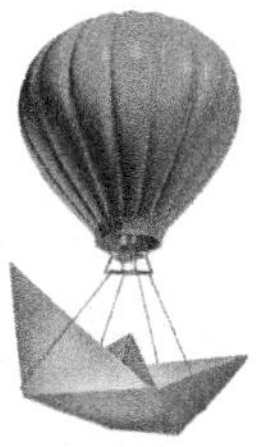

STRATEGY 2 IDENTIFY ALL STAKEHOLDERS: EXPAND THE CIRCLE

TARGET IS SET? Check. Now, to hit our noble goal of saving lives, who is going to need to do something differently? Who do we need to help or influence?

If you have visited Hawaii recently and went shopping, you might have been in for a surprise. The State of Hawaii has banned plastic bags as part of its ecological stance. I discovered this when I reached the checkout with a mound of groceries and nothing to put them in. A helpful clerk said, "No problem, sir. You can purchase one of our reusable bags for just two dollars." Great. Problem solved.

Who were the stakeholders in this change? The Hawaiian citizens and tourists were impacted and needed to adapt. Stores were impacted, too, but also played the role of enabler because they facilitated the change by no longer providing plastic bags and offering an eco-friendly alternative.

The impacted and the enablers. Just two groups to define for any change. This is an easy start to begin developing your change plan. The impacted are those who need to adopt the change. Enablers help them do it — they grease the wheels and clear the way. Like the stores in Hawaii, sometimes enablers are also impacted, needing to adopt the change themselves.

Figure 2.1 presents a simple view of the two basic groups of stakeholders — those who are impacted by the change and those who enable the change. These groups typically overlap.

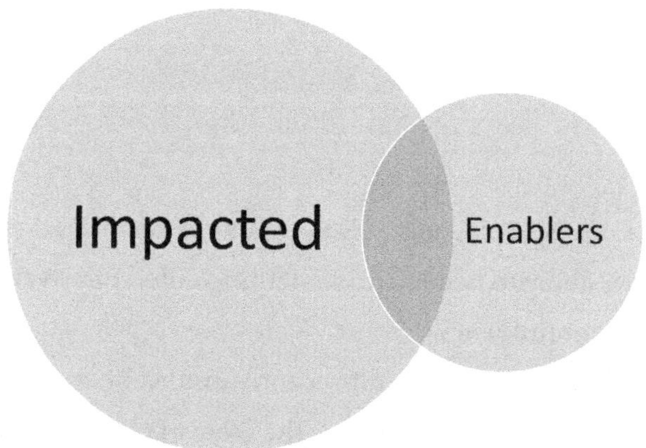

Figure 2.1 Two basic groups of stakeholders: those impacted by change and those who enable change to happen.

In the case of the pandemic, when governments imposed restrictions every enabler was also impacted. Every single person had to adapt in fundamental ways. So, shouldn't it be easy to identify our stakeholders? Not so much.

After twenty-five years of helping organizations identify stakeholders, I'm no longer surprised when someone advises me, "Umm, we forgot about the group of widget inspectors located at our site in Estonia." Often, a missed group is out there somewhere. People who we thought would not be impacted are connected in a way we hadn't considered.

To ensure we develop the right plans for change, we need to look broadly to identify who will feel all the ripple effects. Declaring that the change is for "everyone" is lazy. We must define the different stakeholder groups in detail. Treating everyone the same is a recipe for failure. With that approach, inevitably, a group will be engaged incorrectly, will be unable to adapt, and will end up resisting. That damages credibility for the whole endeavor.

Stakeholder work is foundational for everything we do to move people in a new direction. Identifying all the impacted groups lays the groundwork for our tactical plan.

THE EVIDENCE

In the early days of the pandemic, messaging commonly used the phrase, "We are all in this together." This was a smart approach to make it clear we all had a role to play in this change and in the outcome. Masks, sanitization, social distancing, and eventually vaccines were all meant to protect everyone. But that's where "everyone" ended.

If you were like most people, you read the daily stats on cases and deaths. Reports broke statistics into regions and age groups. We quickly learned that seniors were at higher risk. And, while children could be infected, their symptoms tended to be mild. We looked at national and world maps that used color coding to show us infection hot spots. Latin America was not the place to be in 2020. In 2022, China was not the place to be as the government removed restrictions and infections surged.

Certainly, our healthcare and hospital emergency workers were important stakeholder groups. Communities often identified them as critical resources who deserved special treatment. (I know because my wife is in healthcare, and we enjoyed some generous thank-you meals from appreciative restaurants.)

Parents of young children in school were another important group. How would parents cope with children participating in online learning for the first time? And the kids themselves — how would they handle masks, distancing, and remote learning at such a crucial stage of development?

When vaccination began, the media called out groups with low adoption — often youth and adults who felt invincible but also groups with particular political persuasions and religious beliefs. Now add age, health status, and work environment to uncover additional groups with unique points of view on COVID-19 and what we should do about it.

Millions were forced to stay home, unable to go to work or visit friends. Isolation isn't great for anyone, but it's especially detrimental for those with mental health issues or those who rely heavily on caregivers or a social network for support.

And for employees who would need to work from home, we can further divide those stakeholders into two groups — those who were set up for success and those who were at a clear disadvantage. Some workers already had comfortable home offices, but others would find it extremely difficult to work productively from the kitchen table with children vying for their attention.

So many important groups, and we've barely scratched the surface. We were "all in this together," but we were not all the same when it came to the changes demanded by the pandemic.

IDENTIFY ALL STAKEHOLDERS: THE ANALYSIS

Score: B

"Everyone" was the right approach for marketing the need to save lives, but the strategies and messaging fell short when it came to identifying groups with specific needs and interests related to pandemic-driven changes.

Governments did identify stakeholders, often based on infection rates: the health compromised, aged, children, and frontline care workers. This would be critical to determine impacts and develop targeted change plans for those groups.

Businesses also recognized that the shift in their employees' work environment would not be easy for everyone. In the midst of the pandemic, the World Economic Forum sent a memo to 140 CEOs urging leaders to protect all their stakeholders (not just their shareholders!). The memo included a list of "Stakeholder Principles in the Covid Era":

- Keeping employees safe
- Maintaining fair prices
- Working with governments and offering full support
- Keeping supply chains open

- Maintaining the long-term viability of the company for shareholders

Perhaps most significant is that the reference to shareholders is last on the list, reflecting a growing trend for organizations to broaden the definition of stakeholder to ensure they are mindful of employees, customers, vendors, communities, countries, and the planet.

So, we had a good start at identifying stakeholders, but many other identifiable groups did not come into focus until later. A short list included parents, children, those without a home office, the anxious, and those with particular religious and social beliefs.

In addition, nearly every country experienced a major miss because "everyone" tended to end at the border. Governments put their own interests above others when it came to securing vaccines. I'm not saying that nations did not help one another, just that it was secondary (except in the case of the European Union, which acted as a unified block). Some experts pointed out that "no one is safe until everyone is safe" (Gavi.org).

Low vaccine adoption rates in some areas of the world have helped keep the virus active, enabling its further mutations and spread. That's directly related to nearly all governments' limited view of stakeholders. Helping our neighbors is helping ourselves. "Everyone" cannot end at the border.

Even within countries, knee-jerk reactions had the unintended consequence of punishing citizens. Friends in Australia told me how family members were stranded between states when borders were shut, unable to return home or care for ill and dying family members. For them, it certainly didn't feel like we were all in this together.

The nonprofit news outlet NPR pulled together a raft of findings indicating that closing borders does more harm than good, with the potential to increase racism (NPR.org). Yet, when the Omicron variant appeared, the first response was to close borders and cancel flights between countries, making it difficult for the originating country (South Africa) to bring in the very resources needed to study the variant in depth and advise appropriate health responses. Most people would call that "shooting yourself in the foot."

So, yes, "we are all in this together" when it comes to a global pandemic, but we can't be insular in our interpretation of "we." For the pandemic, looking beyond our country to encompass the world is a critical aspect to achieve the main goal.

While we will look at impact analysis in the next strategy, suffice it to say here that impact work and the resulting change strategy can only be successful based on the foundation of stakeholder identification. At the onset of the pandemic, government and health leaders missed a substantial number of stakeholder groups, and that created gaps in the tactical plan.

As with many programs of change, stakeholder analysis continued throughout the course of the pandemic, aided by growing data sets and advanced modeling tools that identified adoption issues. This ongoing work enabled governments to learn why some groups adapted to this dramatic change faster and identify specific groups that would require more support. While the stakeholder analysis was incomplete at the beginning, our leaders were able to update it and adapt accordingly along the way.

LESSONS FOR CHANGE LEADERS

When identifying stakeholders, using broad groups makes it simple to describe what people need to do to accomplish the goal. But to clarify impacts and plan strategies with specific tactics, we need to tailor our work to groups with different needs. That requires splitting stakeholders into smaller groups according to variations in how they are impacted and how they are likely to respond. For example, a change that is simple for those living in cities might be untenable for those who live in small, rural towns.

When starting your change project, list all the stakeholder groups you can. Start with the two basic groups: the impacted and the enablers. Depending on your project, three large groups — employees, customers, and shareholders — may fit into one or both of those two groups. Next, subdivide or classify groups according to:

- Location
- Language
- Demographics (age, economic status, race, and any other variable that creates distinct groups)
- Political persuasion
- Affiliations and associations
- Culture
- Religion
- Community and social connection
- History and experience

I'm sure you could add a few more factors. Every change is unique and is refracted differently depending on the lens you apply. Identifying smaller groups prevents us from thinking a single approach will capture the attention of all stakeholders equally. It simply will not. What appeals to me and meets my needs will be different from what appeals to you and meets your needs.

The guidance I give to my clients who are leading change is to keep dividing stakeholders into smaller groups as long as there are unique characteristics that may alter their response to the change and their willingness or ability to adopt the change.

Whether updating technology or saving lives, we must look at the ripple effects of change through our primary and secondary stakeholders, including everyone who has a role to play in success — the impacted, enablers, influencers, and influenced. We cannot afford to be limited in our view.

In organizations, look beyond your "borders" to consider customers, clients, communities, lobbyists, suppliers, volunteers, and the person next door to ensure you don't miss any stakeholder groups.

While we essentially only have two basic types of stakeholders — the impacted and the enablers — they come in all shapes and sizes, as shown in Figure 2.2.

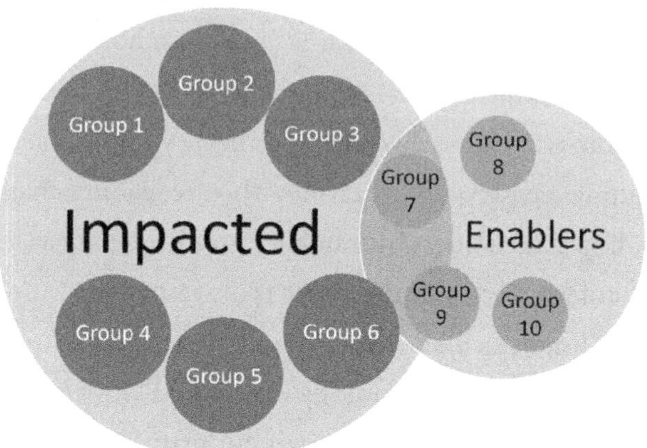

Figure 2.2 Break stakeholders into smaller groups, which helps you to better understand and predict impacts and develop specific strategies to encourage adoption of the change.

It's tempting for every leader to say, "We are all in this together." Use that for messaging, but in practice, take a close look at all the groups needed to make change happen. Make note of those with the power to influence change. Yes, that includes those with the power of authority to enforce change but also consider those with social influence. Who could easily turn the tide of support? Who do people listen to in the crowd? Those are the enablers you want on your side.

TAKEAWAYS FOR YOUR CHANGE INITIATIVE

- Identify broad groups who must adopt the change.
- Follow the ripples of change: who else might be impacted beyond the "borders" of your main stakeholders?
- Break stakeholders into smaller groups primarily by the way the change will impact them. If the change impacts a subgroup differently, split that subgroup into two smaller groups.
- Consider other differentiators that may affect what people need or how they may respond to the change: demographics, location, language, and so forth.
- Identify enablers and influencers: stakeholders who have a role to play in helping others adapt or have influence over others.

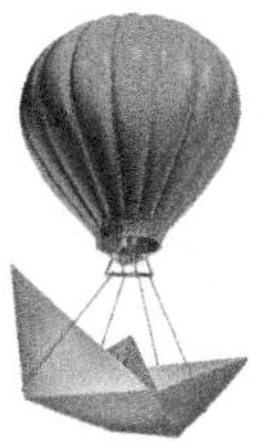

STRATEGY 3 ASSESS IMPACTS: THE HIGHS AND LOWS OF CHANGE

ONE OF MY CLIENTS WAS ROLLING OUT a major financial transformation, which included a host of significant changes throughout the organization. One element would eliminate the task of manually numbering each of the company's thousands of internal projects. Think of it like a product SKU. The company had been using a sequence of numbers and letters signifying cost center, year, and type, among other variables. Employees had inconsistently applied the format for years. This manual process was prone to error, and the mistakes generated a lot of extra work for the IT department.

In contrast, computers are great at numbering! Why not let them assign numbers sequentially, labeling them project number 000001 and proceeding from there? After all, the data contained in the manual project numbers was just a repeat of fields that employees could look up online at any time, as you can see in Figure 3.1. A simple change! Except it wasn't.

Current numbering format

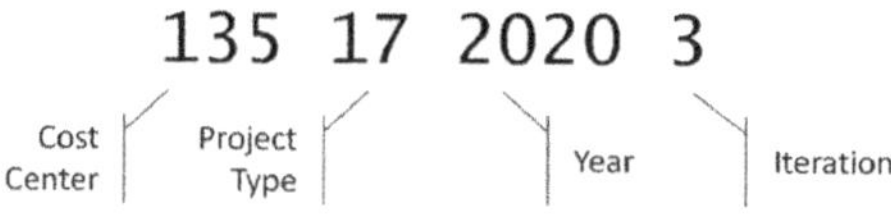

NEW numbering format

00000001

Figure 3.1 The new numbering scheme looked simple, but it wasn't in practice.

Announcing that change triggered a shocking amount of resistance! From engineering to accounts payable we had a boatload of complaints. It seemed that people had learned to read and interpret the existing string of digits in a flash, allowing them to categorize, process, and approve files and invoices in seconds without having to look up the details. Our simple change aimed at eliminating a manual task would double — and in some cases triple — the time it would take employees to finish basic tasks like approving invoices! Whoops.

Judging the correct impact of a change is critical to determine the tactics needed to generate buy-in and compliance. If we rate an impact as low when in fact it is high, we will not invest nearly enough resources to get people to change their behavior. Resistance will kill any chance of success.

Assessing impacts is a blend of art and science. Experience counts for a lot, allowing us to anticipate resistance that a less experienced individual may miss.

THE EVIDENCE

With stakeholders set to "everyone" during the pandemic, leaders had a globe full of people to influence. To save lives, leaders told us we must all wear masks, wash or sanitize our hands a hundred times a day, and social distance (don't socialize with anyone outside of our household and stay six feet away from everyone at all times). Everyone had to do the same thing. But would it be equally easy for everyone?

Let's begin with a simple impact scale:

- Low — It requires minimal adjustment.
- Medium — It will take significant effort to adapt, but it is manageable.
- High — It represents a significant difficulty or a major change to a person's daily routines, requiring challenging adjustments and support.

Now consider our simple rules: mask, sanitize, distance. Each rule on its own is a low impact. It's easy to put on a mask. Sanitizer, when available, is easy to apply. It's easy to stay home and not socialize and stand apart from others, especially from people I don't know.

But what happens when we change the context? How would these rules work in crowded places like the toilet paper aisle in the grocery store? How would we pass objects from one person to another? How would we venture out to shop for food and other necessities? How would we meet our basic human need for social interaction?

We needed more rules for those situations, so our governments imposed additional actions: send kids home from school who come into contact with the virus, close some schools completely, limit stores to a fraction of their typical capacity, and reduce social gatherings to very small groups.

Planning a wedding? You might want to trim that guest list. A lot. Need to get to the gym to keep fit for an upcoming competition? You better book a slot well in advance and limit your workout to an hour.

When change interacts with different needs and environments, those three simple rules begin creating a complex life for:

- Those who cannot wear a mask
- The elderly
- Those who do not drive
- Parents of young kids
- Those needing regular medical care
- Those working in healthcare
- Adult children who regularly visit elderly parents to provide support
- Separated parents who divide childcare responsibilities
- Store owners

No problem! We can expand the do's and don'ts to clarify what people need to do. Many "helpful" lists like the Social Distancing Guidelines chart (Figure 3.2) popped up to make it "easy" to know what to do.

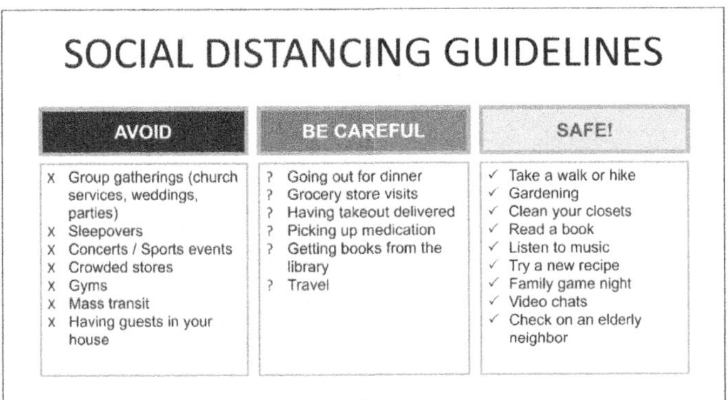

Figure 3.2 Complicated instructions, such as these guidelines for social distancing, can confuse your stakeholders and impede a change initiative.

Well, there you go! With just twenty-two examples in the Social Distancing Guidelines chart, you can figure out how to stay in compliance. But wait, what does it mean to "be careful"? And doesn't "checking on neighbors" violate social distancing? These types of lists emerged everywhere with different examples and interpretations of what was allowable. No one could possibly reconcile them, let alone remember them all.

Consider those who were forced to work from home. No need for masks, sanitization, or social distancing inside the family bubble. This pandemic thing is a snap! Au contraire. I saw people working from their bedrooms, kitchens, and hallways. Some workers used the bathroom for private calls. Ergonomically, it was a disaster. Physically and mentally, they could no longer separate work from home. Boundaries were broken. Some people would feel they never actually left work at the end of the day, which makes it hard to fully disengage, rest, and recharge after a long workday.

This is a recipe for burnout. Figure 3.3 offers a glimpse of the work-from-home issue.

Figure 3.3 Working remotely during the pandemic made it difficult to separate work from home. Where do you go to escape work?

What else? Teams had to adapt to pets and children as regular meeting participants. IT departments had to beef up security for remote workers. In some organizations, the IT departments had to train the entire workforce to use video conferencing tools for online meetings. Teachers needed to adapt hands-on activities to online learning.

Don't forget the kids attending school online. Issues with internet access, lack of laptops, and short attention spans would make it difficult to carry on learning the way they were used to. More ripples.

Understanding that lockdown measures were causing distress, the government of British Columbia took a positive spin by publishing a bingo game containing a variety of self-care activities, such as dancing, laughing, and eating a healthy meal — activities meant to improve coping (GlobalNews.ca). It sparked a major backlash for trivializing what people were feeling into a bingo game. It was clear evidence that government and health leaders had completely misjudged impact by oversimplifying a complicated and stressful behavior change. That misjudgment drove a poor choice of tactics. Navigating this change would require more than a few simple, stress-relieving tactics on a bingo card.

Misstep was a recurring theme. As lockdown measures dragged on and the effects of isolation grew, the buzz of resistance rose quickly. Even some of the most well-adjusted individuals felt the pang of depression. One can only imagine the hell experienced by those already suffering from mental illness.

ASSESS IMPACTS: THE ANALYSIS

Score: C

One could argue that assessing impact was a useless task since the goal of saving lives made all restrictions necessary. Change was mandatory. The alternatives — the likelihood of terrible illness and possibly even death — were not viable options. Most people were willing to step up and comply with the required changes so why bother studying impact?

From the evidence above we see serious problems created by a lack of impact understanding. Oversimplifying the change led to resistance because the three "easy" rules could not and should not be applied in all situations. Assuming everyone would (and could) comply equally led to many problems and complicated recipes that no one could follow.

There is a balance point here. On the one hand, reinforcing the same three basic rules — mask, sanitize, distance — made it simple for everyone. This was easy to remember. That's good.

But on the other hand, while simple, the blanket approach left no room for the needs of specific groups. While the message was simple, the ability to apply the three rules was not equal for all, particularly the elderly, isolated, and disabled. I know two people who have had a lung removed. How do you think they coped with a mask? At the outset, government and health leaders did not provide an exemption for them.

The simple behavioral changes demanded by the goal of saving lives rapidly became complex with numerous caveats and clarifications. Determining the complexity of change — the ripple effects — is a critical skill to assess the true impact of what we are asking people to do. The more complex a change, the more difficult it becomes to comply — even if people want to — and the more likely they are to resist the change. When complexity is high, change leaders need to do more work to encourage and enable adoption. Assessing impact correctly is necessary to devise the right strategies to help your stakeholders navigate change.

The key to getting it right begins with identifying smaller stakeholder groups and their likely reactions (refer to the previous strategy). Analyzing impacts by group (for example, those with a mental illness or reduced lung capacity) would have quickly revealed vulnerabilities and potential friction points that could lead to resistance.

Thankfully, messaging did begin to address these issues. Each day in Alberta, Canada, our local healthcare leader provided an update on the pandemic and then responded to questions about how residents should handle specific situations and how vulnerable groups could cope with restrictions. Alberta's healthcare department granted and explained exemptions. They recorded the questions and answers and posted them online.

What about other groups that were impacted differently? As mentioned, my wife works in healthcare. Authorities were quick to require additional cleaning and contact protocols for healthcare staff. They were ready.

Schools were not. My extended family includes several teachers, and their school systems gave them little support. Adapting lessons to virtual formats and facilitating exercises and tests at a distance was not easy. Many teachers had their own kids at home to monitor at the same time. Technology issues and bandwidth problems contributed to a very difficult transition. Yes, kids were now distanced, but at what cost? We now know it was a very high price.

The day lockdown measures were announced I was delivering a strategy workshop for a continuing care provider (that is, care for the aged in nursing homes). The chief operating officer left during the workshop to enact the company's pandemic plan. This organization had done its homework to assess the impact of a viral outbreak on its residents and was prepared. Deaths were minimal. Other caregivers had not prepared as well, and the consequences were tragic.

When the pandemic struck, governments needed to respond immediately. The short timeframe for change made it impossible to conduct a thorough impact assessment in the moment. Government and health leaders had no idea about how the virus would affect different groups or how long people would need to embrace radical changes. A score of "C" is the best anyone could hope for, given the circumstances.

During the pandemic, the impact assessment had to be an iterative process, and that's what we observed. As time passed, leaders identified additional at-risk groups, clarified exemptions, and put additional supports in place to meet the specific needs of specific stakeholder groups.

LESSONS FOR CHANGE LEADERS

How can we assess the impact of change before we implement that change? I take a very simple approach. Ask yourself these two questions for each stakeholder group:

1. How desirable is the change? More is better. It motivates change.
2. How difficult is the change? More is worse. The more complex the change, the harder it is for people to envision success, which is demotivating. The more difficult it is, the less likely people are to try, and the more likely they are to fail and give up when they do try.

We can use these two questions to form a grid, which helps us identify how people will react and the level of support each group will require (see Figure 3.4). For example, if people see that a change is desirable and easy to accommodate (top-left quadrant), it's likely they will want to adapt and will require little support or encouragement. If they perceive a change has no meaningful benefit and is difficult to navigate (bottom-right quadrant), the probability of resistance is quite high, and we will need to use many more tactics to promote adoption.

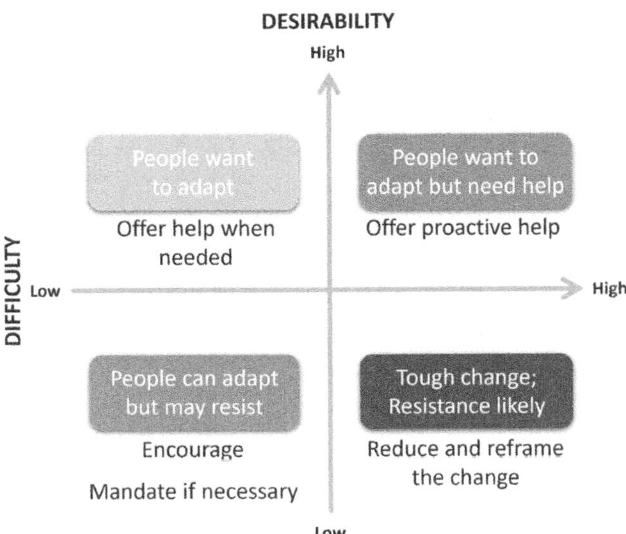

Figure 3.4 As a change leader, you can evaluate impacts and predict ease of adoption by mapping the difficulty of carrying out the change with the desirability of the change.

As a change leader, you must ask these two questions from the stakeholders' perspective — not yours. If you're not sure what various stakeholder groups might think about the change, ask someone who can ably represent each group. With those answers in mind, you can map the groups onto a chart (see Figure 3.5).

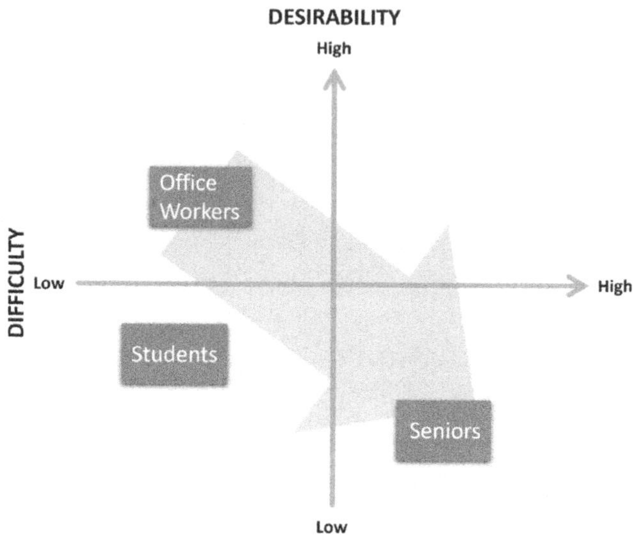

Figure 3.5 This diagram illustrates how three groups were willing or able to adopt change during the pandemic. Placing stakeholder groups on the map allows you to determine the needed support for various stakeholders and select the best strategies to lead your change initiative successfully.

For example, regarding social distancing, you could predict that office workers would regret missing out on hallway conversations with peers, but they would have little difficulty adapting to remote work because of available technology. Many were already familiar with online banking and shopping so working from home would not pose a significant challenge. Most office workers could readily adopt this change.

In contrast, you could predict that seniors, especially those with mobility issues and needing caregiver support, would have the most difficult time with social distancing restrictions. Typically less technically savvy and lacking access to their support network, simply buying groceries and connecting with others could be monumental tasks. For this stakeholder group, adopting this change would be both difficult and undesirable.

Don't stop there. This is just your initial look. Now ask, "What could make this change more difficult for people to adopt?" That thinking often unlocks a number of considerations you might have missed, pushing a change that you first considered to be a low impact to a higher rating of difficulty.

What about the kids who were thrown into online learning from the kitchen table? At first look, we know that most kids are excited about new technology and pick it up quite easily so you could perceive the difficulty as low. But it wasn't easy. Technology was unreliable, this new mode of learning was cumbersome, and kids needed more social interaction as part of their maturing process.

Learning from home would require massive adaptation likely to produce a whole host of easily predicted struggles, making it highly undesirable for most. An initial assessment of low difficulty and high desirability easily moves over to high difficulty and low desirability on a second look. Test scores are now showing just how much children lost during the pandemic years.

As we transition from impact assessment to planning, I want to highlight one important tactic that emerges from the "Difficulty versus Desirability" two-by-two matrix (Figure 3.4). The bottom-right quadrant where desirability is low and difficulty is high presents the toughest change situation. It will be difficult to motivate groups in that zone. Keeping them focused on the end goal can be challenging and even demotivating. To them, it seems impossible to get there. Assuming the change is truly necessary, the best approach for groups in that zone is to reduce the difficulty of the change by breaking it down into smaller steps.

Therefore, to begin, have them focus on accomplishing just the first step. Make it simple and help them succeed. Build them up with consecutive small successes, demonstrating how they are able to progress toward the goal. Changing the focus to just the next step (not the end goal) can help to reduce anxiety dramatically. It's like learning to drive. Trying to remember so many things (signal, steer, shoulder check, mirrors) is overwhelming. A good instructor begins by focusing on one thing: the seating position or the location of each control. Like that instructor, a strong change leader helps people take one step at a time to get them moving toward the final goal.

Taking a structured approach to assess impact enables you to determine the right tactics for each stakeholder group. In the next strategy, we will look at how to develop the tactical plan to successfully implement a change project based on your assessment.

TAKEAWAYS FOR YOUR CHANGE INITIATIVE

- Break large groups into smaller ones if the change impacts them differently (continuing the work of stakeholder analysis).
- For each stakeholder group, ask:
  - Is this a desirable change?
  - Is this a difficult change?
- Map all stakeholder groups onto a "Difficulty versus Desirability" two-by-two grid to clarify their ability and willingness to adopt the change. (Get a helpful tool for this step in the Resources section of my website, www.JeffSkipperConsulting.com.)
- Consider the circumstances that could make the change more difficult for each group, and adjust your impact assessment accordingly.

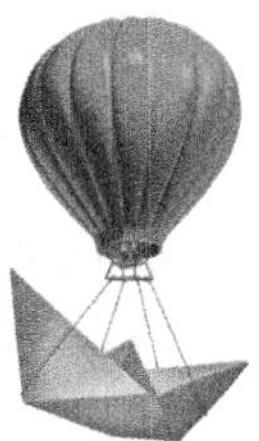

STRATEGY 4
DEVELOP A CHANGE PLAN: A TACTICAL BUFFET

DONE WELL, the impact assessment gives strong clues as to how to best roll out something new. A strong change leader has a toolkit filled with many different ways to inspire commitment to a new set of behaviors to achieve the change. Tactics fall into the following categories:

- Communicate
- Listen and collaborate
- Deploy a network of change agents
- Remove barriers
- Highlight benefits
- Shut down alternatives

THE EVIDENCE

A strong plan for change makes use of all the above tactics in different forms. Let's take a closer look at these six tactical tools in the change toolkit and how government and health leaders used them in the pandemic.

Communicate

Well, you certainly couldn't miss the fact that a pandemic was going on! Headlines raced across every channel of radio and TV and spread like wildfire through social media. Updates were endless — even exhausting — and we were constantly reminded of the consequences for noncompliance.

The message of masking, sanitizing, and distancing was sent out on an endless repeat cycle. Because of the masking mandates, virtually everyone had the experience of being reminded to put on a mask upon entering a store. Oops, back to the car.

Governments set up specific webpages with daily updates and answers to every question received. They provided handy reminder sheets for storefronts: "No mask, no service." "Sanitize on the way in, please."

Businesses adapted by placing helpful circles on the floor: "Stand here." "Move ahead when the next space opens." "Six feet, please!" Apparently, many of us are not good at judging the six-foot social distance guideline so communications included helpful examples:

- The length of a yoga mat
- One alligator
- A hockey stick (very helpful for Canadians)
- Height of a refrigerator
- A Christmas tree
- If you can read these bullets, you're standing too close.

You get the idea. We certainly experienced no shortage of information broadcasted during the pandemic.

Listen and Collaborate

We also did not experience a shortage of opinions about the measures enacted. People raised their voices on the radio, in social media, in city hall, and in front of hospitals. While most were in favor of the changes, others not so much. Were they being heard?

Every day, ministers of health, chief medical officers, presidents, prime ministers, doctors, nurses, and local news reporters responded to those voices. Here are my favorite Q&A items from those early interactions:

- What if my child licks a library book? (Get tested.)
- Will microwaving my mail kill the virus? (No.)
- Can the virus survive in my freezer? (Yes.)
- Can I pick up the virus from a public hand sanitizer? (Yes.)

Government and health leaders were listening to legitimate questions and concerns and responding with the same answers over and over again. This was appropriate because repetition is needed to help people through tough change. During times of stress, we don't always listen well or remember what our leaders are asking us to do.

In work circles, organizations collaborated to solve pandemic problems. A friend of mine leveraged her personal connections with clients to route personal protective equipment from a supplier to a hospital precariously close to running out.

Snipes USA, a chain of about 100 stores, faced an issue common to every retailer: managing the potential for viral spread and disruption in operations. "We absolutely pivoted as an organization and did it in two days," said Jenna Flateman Posner, vice president of digital. They:

- Redirected merchandise from stores to online shipment warehouses.
- Split workers into two groups to isolate potential coronavirus infections.
- Attended the "Covid Sucks Retail Roundtable," a weekly gathering of executives from peer and rival companies who shared tactics to overcome pandemic-related issues.
- Applied software to speed up the online purchase process.
- Kept customers informed about stores' status — whether individual stores were closed, busy, quiet, or implementing restrictions due to infection (NYTimes.com).

Snipes proved that a rapid cycle of change, learn, and adapt could be run and repeated quickly through a collaborative workforce.

Deploy a Network of Change Agents

In the United States and Canada, we love donuts! A lot. It should be considered a primary food group. Every morning, you can see a long line at the donut drive-through. So, what better way to help people than working through the donut industry? In Canada, the government teamed up with our beloved Tim Hortons donut brand to distribute masks with your morning dozen (Edmonton.CTVnews.ca).

Leaders can't be everywhere all at once. When "everyone" is your stakeholder group, you need local help. Partners volunteered in every locale to help healthcare facilities secure needed masks, gowns, and sanitizing resources. We still have a bottle of sanitizer produced by a local brewery — best-smelling sanitizer anywhere! And as pharmaceutical companies rolled out the vaccines, governments worked with drug stores, schools, and healthcare centers to distribute them.

What about inside organizations? In hospitals and nursing homes, healthcare professionals participated in daily huddles to get updates on virus trends and methods to combat spread. They helped to communicate the latest findings and put them into action as agents of change. Those working at the front line also had the opportunity to relay their experiences back up the line, fostering two-way communication. They, too, had influence and were part of the network.

Remove Barriers

The first barrier to change is not knowing what to do. People have questions that demand answers, and we don't all listen to the same channels.

In addition to a plethora of information available on government websites, many local newspapers made their COVID-19 segments free to everyone — no subscription required. Social media platforms helped distribute information but struggled with their role as misinformation multiplied, creating a barrier of confusion, even as they attempted to steer people toward official sources. Doctors who spread untruths were tagged and called out publicly — a necessary reaction in some cases. While it was still possible to get the wrong message, social media platforms made an effort to bring the volume of supporting research from reputable sources to the forefront.

Access to testing could have been a potential barrier, but many governments offered it for free. Hospitals that had the ability opened drive-through options for testing.

Once vaccines became available, the next hurdle was distribution. State and provincial governments opened multiple sites and rolled out vaccinations according to age and medical needs. Lineups and long wait times could have been a barrier for the elderly and infirm. Programmers ramped up appointment systems to alleviate time standing in line.

What if you didn't have a car? "No problem; we provide free public transit to any site." Live too far away from a site? "We have a mobile clinic coming to your area on Tuesday." Don't speak the language? "We will have interpreters available." Unable to leave your facility? "We will be on site." Every barrier had a solution.

What about work-related barriers? Businesses recognized differences in needs for those who were suddenly forced to work at home. They were quick to purchase and ship supplies to their employees. Some received fancy new chairs so they wouldn't wreck their backs working from the couch. Leaders who wanted to learn how to stay connected with their people from a distance could choose from an endless stream of webinars.

And for those who had jobs that could not be performed from home, organizations created policies to keep everyone as safe as possible when working together. Managers quickly drew up protocols to run socially distanced meetings and regularly clean desks, conference rooms, and bathrooms.

We will explore the topic of barriers in more detail in Strategy 8: Enable Change by Removing Barriers.

Highlight Benefits

From the outset, the greatest benefit of adoption was avoiding debilitating illness and possibly death. As we witnessed an ever-growing number of patients at hospital emergency rooms, no one wanted to get sick. When it came to vaccination, government and health leaders made it clear that this was a strong defense against the virus. Vaccination became a passport to activities we desired: shopping, eating out, and travel. That was enough to motivate most people, but not all.

A controversial approach, some governments made benefits tangible by paying people to adapt. California and Louisiana are just two examples of states that offered $100 to get vaccinated. Alberta used lotteries to encourage vaccination. New York offered lifetime hunting licenses. The consensus was that these did not make much of an impact (Bloomberg.com) and wouldn't shift deeply rooted resistance and fear. But these incentives certainly did annoy the people who had already freely stepped up before the states and provinces made those offers.

Rewards can also take the form of avoiding punishment. If you don't comply, what happens? When mask mandates rolled out, resisters could not enter stores (essentially, loss of benefit). That certainly drove a level of adoption.

As vaccination rates slowed, access became an incentive. No vaccine meant no night out at a restaurant, the movie theater, or the mall. Access denied. For some, it meant job loss.

Shut Down Alternatives

If people don't comply and nothing happens, how long do you think a change will last? One of the biggest barriers to change is the ability to get away with noncompliance.

For mask wearing, people had no alternative — everyone had to comply. Rules for compliance were clear (it must be over your nose!), and store employees stationed at the door asked us to comply. Strangers reminded others to put on their masks.

If you returned from visiting a foreign country or tested positive, most countries expected two weeks of isolation. In some countries, officials followed up to ensure individuals were, in fact, isolating, effectively shutting down alternatives.

The true test of compliance came when businesses instituted vaccination as a requirement for work. Without question, organizations' vaccine mandates drove huge spikes in adoption.

Some employees tried to work around it. The Calgary Police Service won the right for its employees to present daily negative test results instead of getting vaccinated, and the city had to pay for those tests. Once that door was opened, others took the same route, and all city workers gained the right to have their employer pay for daily negative tests. As a taxpayer, I was effectively paying to enable an entire workforce to be noncompliant. How do you think this affected my own desire to comply?

Some businesses offered alternatives to vaccination: work from home. Caught between a desire to support vaccination and fear of constructive dismissal claims or loss of key personnel, businesses accommodated workers by eliminating contact with customers and peers. Other companies stuck with broad mandates and simply planned to deal with the loss of staff.

DEVELOP A CHANGE PLAN: THE ANALYSIS

Score: B

Pandemic change plans included every type of tactic, and governments applied them liberally throughout the pandemic. Some tactics were hampered by poor stakeholder and impact analysis at the outset. You can communicate as much as you want, but if the safety guidelines are confusing, change will be evasive.

Nevertheless, governments utilized the entire toolkit of tactical options with varying degrees of success. The point is that they took a multifaceted approach — exactly what is necessary during a truly disruptive change.

LESSONS FOR CHANGE LEADERS

Executives and project managers ask me what they need to do to lead their people when promoting a major transformation. Once we complete stakeholder and impact assessments, it's easy to draft a plan drawing upon the change levers discussed in this strategy.

Communication is the most critical intervention. It underpins all the others. Without information, people cannot act. And the thirst for information during change remains high throughout the change process. Stress drives the search for answers. Every program of change requires a steady cadence of communication, even when you don't have anything new to report.

Communication often contains a high proportion of repetition. We don't want stakeholders wondering what to do; we want them to know exactly what to do so they can take action with zero hesitation. That requires relentless reinforcement through clear communication.

Therefore, your plan for change must include a clear timeline for communication outlining key messages, the sender, and the channel. Aim for variety. Your audience needs to hear the message in different ways from different sources since not everyone is tuned into the same channel. Ensure key messages continue to highlight the benefits along the way. Not every benefit will appeal universally so vary the benefits you spotlight.

Your analysis of stakeholders will have revealed enablers. Consider how you can engage them as fellow communicators and agents of change. In the simplest arrangement, you can ask them to share information as part of the communication plan. I prefer to set them up as representatives of the program with the ability to run demonstrations, make presentations to local teams, and set up calls with project sponsors when questions get difficult.

You can rely on enablers to take the pulse of the organization and inform you about the sentiment toward the change. They can actively identify potential hotspots of resistance in groups that you, as the change leader, can't easily reach. This, of course, enables them to listen and collaborate, but don't rely solely on your agents.

Change leaders need to get into the trenches and talk directly with those impacted by change. I've sent many executives into tough groups to facilitate a conversation. They always come back thankful for the opportunity to learn and gain insight, and they are motivated to take action that will best serve their stakeholders.

In terms of shutting down alternatives, consider what you can remove or put in place to prevent people from reverting to old behaviors. Can you identify anything in the environment that would suggest previous ways of working are still acceptable? For example, if you want your employees to use a new process, remove the old training guides and instruction sheets. Get rid of an old form when a new one is rolled out. Plan to shut the "back door" all at once or gradually over time, depending on the approach that best suits your goal and the confidence level of your stakeholders.

I must add one caveat: Assume your plan will change. Sometimes dramatically. As you will see in Strategy 6, people are not entirely predictable. You don't know exactly how everyone will react. Think of your change plan as a draft that you must constantly revise in real time as you progress through the change initiative. It's a living document.

With a well-defined goal and plan in hand, you are ready to put your change plan into practice. First decision: who will lead the change? Find out in the next strategy.

TAKEAWAYS FOR YOUR CHANGE INITIATIVE

- Tactics are only as good as the stakeholder and impact assessment that precedes them.
- Use all the levers:
  - Communicate early and often using many different channels.
  - Listen to your stakeholders and answer their questions.
  - Collaborate with peers and partners who can help.
  - Deploy a network of change agents to reinforce messaging and identify potential problems.
  - Remove barriers to compliance.
  - Highlight benefits and remind stakeholders about the consequences of noncompliance.
  - Shut down alternatives.
- Respond to or take away every possible reason for noncompliance.
- Modify tactics as you monitor how stakeholders react to them.

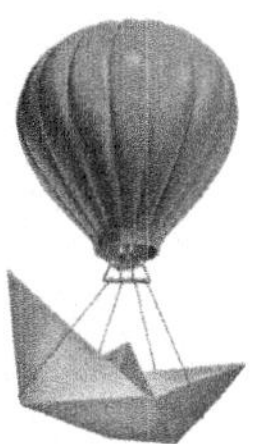

STRATEGY 5
LEAD THE CHANGE: AVOID DIVIDED LOYALTIES

WHY DO BEER COMMERCIALS feature likeable people doing interesting things? Every change needs an attractive face, someone you can relate to. Part of our decision to adopt a change is based on determining whether we can actually do it. Seeing people who are similar to ourselves or who we look up to taking the lead increases the chances we will be convinced we can do it, too. People help bring the change to life.

Therefore, selecting the right leader for a change is critical. If your stakeholders think a change is good but the process is led by someone they do not trust, they are unlikely to follow.

THE EVIDENCE

When the pandemic hit the news, the most common faces to see were chief medical officers and representatives from the department or ministry of health. Good choice. They are experts. The problem? There were too many experts:

- National experts
- State/provincial experts
- City experts
- Doctors
- Nurses
- Homeopathic advisors
- Talk show hosts

In general, these experts were all saying the same thing, repeating the mantra: mask, sanitize, distance, vaccinate. Those who disagreed were called out, and their opinions were refuted with science. The national and state/provincial experts updated and reinforced findings regularly, doing their best to keep the flow of science-based information coming.

But another class of leaders was also involved: politicians. Every good leader should publicly endorse a change that is good for everyone. His or her support can be a strong, deciding factor for many people. In the best cases, politicians stood behind their medical representatives — literally, in some cases — to show their support. They bowed to the authority of the expert.

The trouble is that, for politicians, endorsement can actually sway some people in the opposite direction. Nowhere was that more pronounced than in the United States where masks and vaccination became politicized, and compliance came to be seen as a statement of support for one party or the other. This was also wrapped up in the way political leaders expressed support. President Trump introduced confusion several times. President Biden came across as an overbearing parent with mandates and an enemy of rights. Lines were quickly drawn.

In general, pandemic leaders walked the talk, complying with the rules and getting vaccinated early. But some did not. Evidence of leaders, such as UK Prime Minister Boris Johnson, in gatherings without practicing social distancing or wearing masks went viral. If leaders wouldn't comply with the rules and adopt the change, why should anyone else? Leaders are constantly scrutinized and must walk the talk. A few mistakes can undo months of strong efforts to convince people to change.

We must consider one more group of leaders: celebrities, local heroes, and influencers. For me, when Tom Hanks publicly announced that he and his wife had contracted the virus, it really hit home that this pandemic was real. Tom is highly credible, and he spoke openly about his symptoms. And then so did Idris Elba and Dwayne Johnson (The Rock). The list of celebrity testimonials grew long, with each one posting about their experience and encouraging people to comply with the rules, get tested, and get vaccinated.

Some did not make it. We lost Colin Powell, Cloris Leachman, Ellis Marsalis, Jr., Charley Pride, and many others. While we mourn the loss of life, these highly publicized deaths helped to reinforce the consequences of noncompliance. They reinforced "what's in it for me," which is key to changing behavior. While all lives are equally important, there is no doubt that influencers have a substantial influence on the public. Each celebrity testimonial — whether in life or in an announcement of their death — had the power to change minds. They were the enablers of change.

LEAD THE CHANGE: THE ANALYSIS

Score: D

If all the people leading the change are saying the same thing, that's great! For the pandemic, we had too many leaders with too many variations in the message. With states and provinces having the latitude to encourage and enforce compliance as they saw fit, many differences in messaging and requirements arose, all of them extremely visible.

Communication does not know borders, and the mixed messages created confusion when experts in one region declared the need for lockdown, while experts elsewhere declared an end to lockdown according to different criteria. Government and health leaders could have done a much better job coordinating messages across our regions. Even organizations could not agree, with some applying vaccine mandates while others did not.

These differences added up to a growing distrust in both leaders and science. How can immutable science lead to different conclusions and different actions? Dr. Anthony Fauci in the United States had the toughest time with that challenge, having to change his message as new findings emerged — from no masks required to masks required, and even having to contradict a president. His credibility took a hit, as did many others who had to reverse course.

To those who work in science, this is unsurprising. Conclusions improve as sample sizes increase and as scientists repeat studies over time. We are always learning. At the beginning, leaders were acting quickly on whatever data they had available, which was not much. When trying to save lives, actions tended to be extreme (lockdowns, closing borders, mandatory isolation) even with limited data. The risk of getting it wrong was too great to take tentative measures. Those who waited were criticized.

This leads us to an important lesson about leadership during change. Because leaders make mistakes, there will be times when they must admit publicly that they got it wrong. Dr. Deena Hinshaw, Alberta's Chief Medical Officer of Health, was heralded as a strong tower during the pandemic. She provided daily updates and responded to endless questions, all with a calm tone that invited confidence. Until she messed up.

Dr. Hinshaw laid out an aggressive plan to fully reopen businesses based on vaccination rates. The province hit the target, and Alberta was declared "open for summer" with restrictions removed. People rejoiced. They traveled, attended concerts, and participated in all kinds of summery events. Then numbers surged, and they kept climbing. Alberta reinstated its COVID-19 measures. Dr. Hinshaw made a clear, heartfelt apology. Alberta had moved to get back to normal too quickly. She had made an error. Previously, she had failed to communicate clearly, but now she wholeheartedly conveyed, "I am sorry."

Arrogance does not win awards. A bit of vulnerability makes leaders more relatable. I must give points to President Biden for going door to door to talk with residents about vaccination in areas where people expressed some of the most hesitation. It's much more difficult to deny a leader who takes the time to speak with you personally, let alone the President. This is leading from the front.

LESSONS FOR CHANGE LEADERS

Consistent messaging during disruption is critical. When programs of change are complex, I've heard leaders suggest that they split the sponsorship role among two or more people. After all, leading a change program does take significant time.

Don't do it. It's a terrible idea. Who are people supposed to listen to? Splitting leadership creates opportunities for conflicting messaging. Worse, it communicates that no one person is willing to take full accountability for the change. It is appropriate for a leader to be backed by a committee of experts and support personnel, but you should present only one face to your stakeholders.

Beyond your primary change leader, every other leader in an organization also has a role to play in reinforcing messages and ensuring change is applied and sticks at the local level. Too often, organizations do not make this clear with their middle managers. We assume middle management will fall in line and figure out what to say. That's a mistake. Everyone applies their own filters. We have to be specific about what we want every leader to say and do to ensure they are 100 percent aligned with the direction set at the top. The top person retains ultimate accountability. He or she delegates responsibility for making the change happen to leaders and agents throughout the organization.

The pandemic also demonstrated how important it is for leaders to be seen, especially to be seen walking the talk. Visibility during a change effort helps us to connect with the leader, trust that person, and learn how to translate directions into action. Walking around the office is not enough (especially in a hybrid workforce). One-on-one conversations with various stakeholders are instrumental in informing the change leader about how well the change is going, where resistance is beginning to surface, and what the leader needs to adjust in the plan.

We cannot forget the role of influencers. Every organization has them, and they often exist outside of the hierarchical power structure. They may even live outside of the organization. You would have identified these influencers when you reviewed the stakeholders of the change. Consider your influencers as a potential part of your unofficial leadership team or change agents during complex change.

Leaders do not always get it right. They make mistakes, have to go back on their promises, and shift the scope of the change. At the outset of your change plan, set the expectation that the plan will move a bit here and there. The intent is to limit the amount of shifting, but we all know that surprises and new information will show up in any significant disruption. Leaders bear the responsibility of making agile adjustments to the change plan as they roll it out over time, as we will see in the next strategy.

TAKEAWAYS FOR YOUR CHANGE INITIATIVE

- Choose a leader who has credibility with your stakeholder groups.
- Change needs a single leader (sponsor) with final accountability for its implementation.
- Other leaders endorse the sponsor, reinforcing the message without alteration.
- Leverage influencers like celebrities and local heroes to lend additional support.
- Ensure leaders lead by example and are visibly doing so.
- Personal contact and dialogue between the top leader and those to be influenced make a big difference.
- Set the expectation that messages and direction may shift as you begin implementing the change and learning more about what works.
- When mistakes happen apologize, explain what happened, and commit to do better.

STRATEGY 6
EXECUTING THE PLAN IS REVISING THE PLAN

WE KNOW THE TARGET, the audience, the impacts, and the plan. With a leader in place, it's time to make it happen!

In theory, this is the easy part. The change team drafts the messages, and the leader stands up and does his or her thing. The program takes its first steps, and hopefully, the change gains momentum. But it doesn't always work that way. We need to adapt tactics in real time as stakeholders react.

Think of it like a recipe for a pie you've been making your entire life. You know what to do. You will mix apples and sugar for the filling, flour and butter for the crust. You will make adjustments depending on how the taste and consistency come together. Sugar . . . needs just a bit more. Perhaps add cinnamon to give it some spice.

The same applies to our change levers — our tactical buffet. We need them all in varying doses. They are part of every change plan, and so we bake them in. Then we pull more from each category as the situation demands. Vaccination for COVID-19 is a perfect example. In most countries, behavior change (compliance) surged as people lined up to get their first dose. Leaders were relieved. And then demand dropped. People stopped coming. The initial tactics stopped working. Back to the toolkit for a bigger batch of a key tactic: remove barriers.

THE EVIDENCE

For the pandemic, the tactical plan remained consistent throughout: reinforce the need to mask, sanitize, distance, and vaccinate. Leaders emphasized these elements in different ways as the pandemic progressed through the stages of initial lockdown through each of the variants. The degree of the required change shifted over time.

Consider social distancing rules. As cases ebbed and surged, leaders applied distancing rules on a sliding scale. As positive cases grew, distancing guidelines became more stringent, and communication ramped up to emphasize safe practices to reduce the spread. Message repetition increased. As vaccination rates increased, leaders limited these guidelines only to the unvaccinated, which also shifted the reward structure. This worked to increase vaccinations further.

When you execute your change plan and find you need to adjust tactics, it's important to consider two critical factors: the role of culture and the power of resistance.

The Role of Culture

Business author Peter Drucker is famously quoted as saying, "Culture eats strategy for breakfast." You need look no further than the pandemic for evidence of that truth.

In New Zealand, lockdown was rapid and complete. No one in or out. Citizens had voted in Prime Minister Jacinda Ardern to get things done, and she did. She made decisive actions in line with her government's mandate, and people complied. Yes, there was friction, but it was a working strategy to keep the virus out. The island culture paid off.

Sweden was on the opposite end of the scale, taking a generally hands-off approach and relying on herd immunity, which seemed to suit its social culture very well.

And of course, the United States — where personal rights and freedoms are paramount — foundered in its attempts to drive high vaccination rates after a strong start. Mandates made it worse. Culture ruled the day.

While change leaders must factor culture into the assessment of impact, it can appear in surprising ways and can force a change in strategy along the way. Ignore it at your peril.

The Power of Resistance

People don't like to be told what to do. When infection rates began to drop, businesses, such as Tesla and JPMorgan Chase, were quick to tell employees they would be expected to return to the office. The resistance to this news was tangible. With low levels of unemployment, employees declared their willingness to look for greener pastures if they weren't allowed to keep the flexibility of remote work with its huge benefit of time saved. (No commute!) Jamie Dimon, CEO of JPMorgan Chase, eventually admitted that 40 percent of his employees will have a hybrid work arrangement, a major reversal of his tough stance. This is not to say that you must give in to resistance. Read Strategy 9 for guidance on how to respond to resistance positively.

EXECUTE THE PLAN: THE ANALYSIS

Score: A

One of the most interesting aspects about the change driven by the pandemic was the expected response time. In typical change programs, we set a target date for implementation that may be months or years in the future. For the pandemic, the runway was weeks, if not days. When the Omicron variant surfaced, nations shut their borders within hours.

This extraordinarily fast response time is an important point for a number of reasons. First, it proved that large organizations (in this case, governments) could pivot very quickly if sufficiently motivated. Second, it demonstrated that people could adapt much faster than we normally would expect. Self-interest ("you might die") is a strong motivator.

Governments' speed of response coupled with the speed of adapting the tactics as new research emerged earns high marks. However, rapid change often leaves some gaps. In Canada, for instance, the government mandated that every person arriving from a foreign country would be tested, effective immediately. Forty-eight hours after the announcement, airport officials still had no information about how to apply this new mandate at their airports. This surprise announcement completely took them off guard.

In a similar glitch, the US mandated negative tests no more than twenty-four hours prior to boarding a plane with a US destination. At that time, most test results were delivered in a three-day window. Passengers' ability to meet the requirement was questionable.

A friend of mine works for the taxation arm of the Canadian government and said she often got updates faster by watching the news rather than relying on internal communications.

Rapid change is good, but coordination is critical.

LESSONS FOR CHANGE LEADERS

This strategy is intended to reinforce just one point: change planning is iterative. The plan is always in motion because you cannot completely predict how people will respond. The levers of change presented in Strategy 4 remain in play, but you need to alter the mix as you act and observe responses. Also, as noted earlier, this is when you may become aware of stakeholder groups that you missed in the original analysis. It's normal. Assess the impact to those groups now, and adjust the plan as needed.

With all this potential editing of the plan, do you really need one? Can you lead change by the seat of your pants? Don't get me wrong — planning is necessary! Stick to the plan. Change leaders select specific actions to achieve a specific outcome, and those actions are intended to be comprehensive, with many tactics running in parallel. Adjustments are usually incremental rather than revolutionary.

When motivation is flagging, focus on the benefits of change. If resistance is rising, leverage your leaders and influencers to engage in dialogue, listen to the resisters' concerns, and respond accordingly. Shift your communication activities as timelines adjust. Highlight success stories, and add quotes from people who really "get it" to enhance your messages.

Every change plan must be agile. Change plans never remain static. To determine when to make these adjustments, we need data.

Measurements are critical, and we will explore them in more detail in Strategy10.

Next, we will take a deeper dive into some of the most interesting and challenging tactics applied: communicating effectively and removing barriers.

TAKEAWAYS FOR YOUR CHANGE INITIATIVE

- Put the plan into action.
- Take your culture into account, as it can be a major reason for resistance or support.
- Coordination is key during complex change: expect gaps when moving quickly.
- Monitor indicators of success and resistance.
- Adjust the plan to adapt.
- Revisit the stakeholder and impact assessment, if needed, to adjust assumptions and add or further define groups.

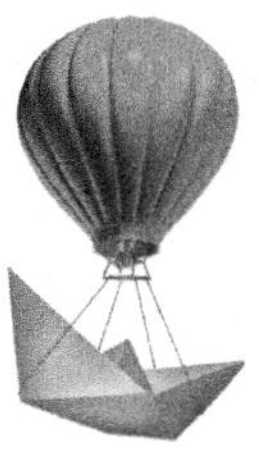

STRATEGY 7 COMMUNICATE EFFECTIVELY: TOO MUCH DATA AND NOT ENOUGH WISDOM?

EVERYONE SAYS, "You can never communicate too much." Everyone is wrong. Communication is a skill requiring a high degree of competence and a sharp sense of timing. Blitzkrieg will get the message out, but we need finesse to inspire adoption. Boring messages get tuned out over time. When no one is listening, we cannot achieve change.

THE EVIDENCE

"This is an urgent health message." A single sentence that conjures the worst scenarios in your mind.

Had the zombie apocalypse finally come? The instructions that followed would certainly have you think so. In 2020, we crowded around my wife's phone to hear what our medical leaders had to say about this new virus originating in the East.

While the interpretation of what was happening and what we should do varied somewhat, the communication was clear about the most important elements:

- Contagious and deadly virus
- Keep your distance from others
- Flatten the curve
- We are all in this together

Repetition ensued. Security at store entrances reinforced the rules. Signs were everywhere. Message received!

Regular communication from our leaders was beneficial. Every news source had a dedicated space for COVID-19 information, making it easy to get the latest updates on what was happening.

But as the pandemic raged on and variants emerged, we began drowning in data — and interpretation. Study results appeared regularly, some from questionable sources using questionable research techniques. It became difficult to make sense of it all. The noise on social media was deafening. What was truth?

In such an environment, opinions diverged radically. One of my favorite quotes: "A single symptom, such as a runny nose, is a near daily thing for many allergy sufferers, perpetually grubby children, and basically anyone who goes for a walk in the cold," wrote Canadian journalist Sabrina Maddeaux. "Treating every sneeze like a DEFCON-level threat simply doesn't pass the smell test this far into the pandemic. To do so is nonsensical bordering on hysterical, and it risks further undermining fragile public trust" (NationalPost.com).

And that's exactly what happened. Regular channels for communications lost credibility. With vaccinations rising, why weren't we removing restrictions? In France, Canada, and other countries, protests got out of hand. Leader communications kept coming, but they lacked any acknowledgment of what science was beginning to make clear: the time had come to ease up on restrictive pandemic measures.

COMMUNICATE EFFECTIVELY: THE ANALYSIS

Score: B

During the pandemic, we experienced an onslaught of communication — most of it helpful. The tone was appropriate to the gravity of the developing situation. Government and health leaders demonstrated a few important guidelines — set a cadence, get above the noise, chart a course with hope, make it personal, and tell stories.

Set a Cadence

When change is difficult, we need a regular infusion of information. In terms of the pandemic, this was never an issue. There was no shortage of information, updated on a daily basis. Many of us tuned into daily emails or podcasts to get the latest numbers.

I am frequently asked by senior leaders, "How often should we meet with our people during the change?" I advise them to pace communication to the needs of the situation and the workforce. When stress is high, people need more communication, not less — even if there is nothing new to say. Just hearing that leaders are on top of things and no major problems have arisen can have a positive effect. As people adapt and the situation stabilizes, meetings can be less frequent.

Get above the Noise

The main problem during the pandemic was the relentless campaigns of misinformation. For every study that confirmed the validity of vaccines, ten people started chains of antagonistic posts aimed at discrediting research by quoting outliers, generalizing from uncommon experiences, or relying on the validation of like-minded resisters amplified by social media algorithms.

With all that noise, it was difficult to sort truth from opinion or fiction. One analyst observed that many people struggled to analyze competing messages because they are bad at math and cannot understand graphs. He's not wrong. We assume people can assess charts for merit, but, without the skills to discriminate information sources and biases, people are easily led in the wrong direction. That suggests an intervention that was not widely used: teaching people how to test the truth.

Most people don't know:

- Who the trusted sources of information are and where to find them
- How to interpret statistics and graphs
- How we are persuaded to untenable positions

The only way to combat these issues is to teach people how to judge what they see and hear. But who wants to take a basic course in statistics? Blech. Who wants to listen to a podcast on how to amaze your friends with graphs? Hmm, maybe.

I realized my own perspective about COVID-19 was shaped by the news sources I frequented, including the BBC for world news, CBC for Canada, and both The New York Times and The Washington Post for the United States. While they have their own biases and make periodic mistakes, these traditional media outlets have a high degree of credibility for providing valid information.

By contrast, social media — where most people look for information — is the Wild West of information where truth is crowd-sourced and the efforts of Facebook and Twitter to control the spread of harmful information were woefully inadequate. Since social media algorithms are widely perceived to be biased, why not swing the bias to blatantly promote information from verified sources over everything else? Social media organizations did begin doing so, but in the first two years of the pandemic it was too little too late. The damage had been done.

The fight to discredit misinformation (bleach cocktail anyone?), bad science ("once infected always immune"), and conspiracy theories ("COVID-19 is spread via 5G network") was endless, but it was a necessary fight to keep people focused on the required change. Pandemic leaders made efforts here, but the fight to bring accurate, reliable communication to the forefront needed a stronger team and more pressure on social media leaders.

In addition to a regular infusion of credible information in your change project, you can complement your messaging with a completely different, creative, and eye-catching approach. Take a journey with me to Niagara Falls on the border between Canada and the United States. Can you hear the roar as 160,000 cubic meters of water drop 50 meters every minute to crash on the rocks below? It's an awe-inspiring sight and really, really loud.

One night, staff at the nearby Marriott worked out a way to display a great-big heart on the side of their building by leaving the lights on in certain rooms left vacant as travel restrictions destroyed their business. That heart was an inspiring sight in itself, but within twenty-four hours it was no longer alone. Hearts appeared on the side of every hotel above the falls, above the noise. With lights, the employees of the hospitality industry shouted their praise for our healthcare workers.

In our city, mail carriers arranged drive-bys at hospitals where they honked their thanks to our medical first responders. Citizens hung hearts outside nursing home windows.

My point? As a change leader, you need to get creative to get above the noise.

Chart a Course with Hope

Even the strongest among us gets tired of having to do things differently. We want things to go back to the way they were, and this leads to resistance. Leaders were caught at parties with no social distancing. Grandparents boldly traveled to visit their grandkids.

Maintaining compliance with change requires hope that things will get better. Hope that we will get more adept at working with the change. Or hope that the transition will be over soon and our environment will shift to conditions that we will find easier. Being able to envision a better future creates hope that keeps us motivated.

With that in mind, governments held out hope that at some point the lockdown would end. But when? We needed a plan, so leaders created visuals to make it clear when various aspects of our lives would shift to a more comfortable setting (see Figure 7.1). Just like the big thermometers that show how donations progress toward a major goal, we watched the numbers to see when we could trash the masks. Remember, people naturally strive toward achievable goals.

THE COVID-19 PATH TO RECOVERY

Transition	Stage 1	Stage 2	Stage 3
25% vaccinated/immune	50% vaccinated/immune	65% vaccinated/immune	75% vaccinated/immune
• Limits on gatherings remain • Health measures/ restrictions in effect • Easing of restrictions only once metrics acheived	• May raise group meeting size • May increase store capacity limit • Masking & distancing rules remain • Isolation protocols remain	Potential to shift to: • No restrictions • Large entertainment events can proceed • Masking & distancing encouraged • Isolation protocols remain	Potential to shift to: • Resumption of in-class education for K-12 • No masks • No isolation

Figure 7.1 Clear milestones toward a better future provide hope and motivation. When planning your change initiative, chart the milestones along the path toward the end goal.

Make It Personal

I studied many messages sent by organizations during the pandemic. Some came across very cold — PayPal merely reminded people about how to use its service — while others were extremely sympathetic and inspiring. Here is a portion of a message from Don Smitten, the president of the Alberta Motor Association:

> This long weekend, many Albertans will reflect on the power of sacrifice for the greater good. It's an idea with profound relevance during this pandemic, when barren public spaces remind us of what we're all giving up to keep each other safe.

> Each of us is being asked to prioritize lives over livelihood, community over self, to flatten the curve of COVID-19. It's a weighty reminder of how deeply we're all connected, and how easily our actions can affect those around us . . . . Everywhere I look, Albertans are using this time to care for one another — from checking on their elderly neighbours, to delivering groceries to the vulnerable, to plastering windows with paper hearts to boost community spirit. Our members are looking for the good and embracing the simpler things in life. Homemade baking is being left on friends' doorsteps. Children are discovering the joys of pen pals. Extended families are sharing meals over video conference. And through it all, I'm happy to see people are also being kind to themselves — doing little things that make a big difference in emotional wellbeing. I finally understand why dogs get so excited over a simple walk or drive; it's about feeding the soul . . . . So whether it's playing a board game with family, treating yourself to an indulgent dessert, watching an uplifting video, or taking the car a few extra miles while you're out for essential business anyway, I encourage you to do something this weekend that nurtures your spirit. We're all in this together (AMA.AB.ca).

Mr. Smitten wrote these extremely powerful and personal messages regularly (cadence!), which truly inspired us to keep complying with safety guidelines while taking care of ourselves.

The Alberta government created a plan that made it clear how each person could play a role in getting the economy back on track.

The goal was to get vaccinations to a level that would allow our province to host the Calgary Stampede — a massive annual international attraction — in July 2020. It would be a big party so get vaccinated!

That personal call to help achieve the goal did drive vaccinations. Combining an incentive to each person to contribute toward the goal, along with the promise of a desirable future, merged a sense of personal control with the motivation of hope.

Shared goals also reinforced that we were all in this together, leveraging peer pressure to keep people in compliance. No one wanted to be a barrier to removing restrictions. It was personal but also communal.

Tell Stories

"Do you know anyone who has had the virus?" I was quite taken aback when a friend asked me that early in 2020, inferring that perhaps the threat was not real. In my case, while I had not been up close and personal with the virus, people in my close network had already lost parents to COVID-19. The threat was real for me. I had heard their stories. The question demonstrated how people are often motivated by their personal connection to a change. Stories, or a lack thereof, have the power to strengthen or weaken that connection.

When celebrities and influencers began talking about their experiences, it helped to make the situation real. News channels zoomed in on patients who had been close to death, urging people to get vaccinated. Long COVID gave us another perspective that sometimes illness doesn't go away on the schedule we want. As I write this, an email just arrived from The Washington Post with the headline: "Long COVID is destroying careers, leaving economic distress in its wake." Who wants that as their future?

Stories convey and elicit emotional responses (fear, disgust, anger, hope), which drive action more readily than stats. We become immune to the numbers, but it's hard to discount the story of someone we know or can relate to. People make it real. Stories about people just like you and me helped us to connect with the seriousness of the situation. Government reps and news channels used stories liberally.

LESSONS FOR CHANGE LEADERS

In the midst of difficult change, most people feel like life has become chaotic and out of control. That drives stress and triggers the fight-or-flight response that hinders adaptation. Lack of action may be interpreted as active resistance when it is often just fear. Effective communication is about more than keeping people informed. It can encourage and inspire people to push through the stress. Done right, it fosters a sense of control by giving people the details and motivation they need to take action.

Because change makes the future uncertain, stakeholders are hungry for information that will help predict what will happen next. Regular communication satisfies that need. If we don't deliver, they will look for answers elsewhere, often in the wrong places. Leaders should fill in the gaps before people start making it up for themselves.

As part of your change tactics, plan a regular cadence of communication through an email newsletter, live calls, and other channels. Develop a brand for your communications so people can easily identify email newsletters and other announcements in their inboxes. Give it a snappy title, and keep the message succinct. That's why my weekly newsletter always contains "[IMPACTED]" in the subject line. You can't miss it.

When your stakeholders know they will always hear an update every Tuesday or on the first day of the month, this helps make the future predictable. It provides structure that promotes calm. Even if you have no real news to report at the next update, a steady rhythm reinforces that the lines of communication are open, and leaders aren't hiding anything.

That same cadence accompanied by a clear plan for the entire change process also fosters a sense of control. Milestones add a layer of structure over what can feel like chaos at times during the change. (See Figure 7.2 as an example.) Order makes things predictable and reduces anxiety. Milestones act as markers along the trail. We can't see the end goal, but we know as long as we stay on the path and keep the markers in sight, we will get there.

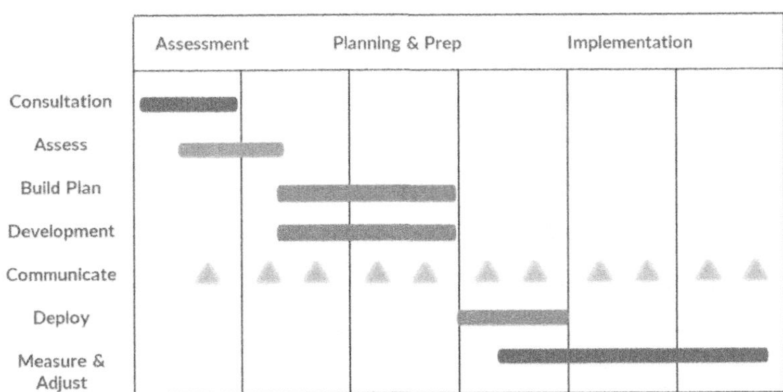

Figure 7.2 Providing a clear plan for change with regular milestones brings order to chaos. Notice the regular cadence of communication from start to finish during this change initiative.

Strong communicators never leave it up to the audience to find their messages in a single location. Use many channels and innovative, attractive approaches to get above the noise. In organizations, email is the most used and the most ignored channel. It's easy to miss the change leader's critical communication unless it stands out. Important messages must be both verbal and written. I've seen change initiatives include internal podcasts, posters in bathrooms, and virtual backgrounds on conference calls. This ensured no one could say, "I didn't know what was going on." Run contests, and give out prizes. Get creative so you will be heard above the noise.

Here's a creative solution: I was leading the rollout of a major transformation for a client, and we needed to be sure field personnel knew what to do. They were not regular users of email. A team member suggested we put key messages on air fresheners and distribute them for their trucks. Brilliant! She followed this up by sending basic instructions for a new process that field personnel could print and clip onto the trucks' sun visors. These were a big hit.

While you want your communication to follow a cadence, boring and unchanging messages get lost with the constant bombardment of messages we all receive on a daily basis. In addition to using creative approaches to make your message attractive, consider leveraging your enablers and influencers. Successful organizations use enablers and influencers from within and outside their companies to mix things up and sway opinion. This is most effectively accomplished through stories.

When leaders convey stories with emotional impact, it moves people to act. These don't always have to be real stories — they can be carefully constructed visions of a reasonable future that portrays how lives are made better: "Picture if you will . . . ." Every change has an eventual connection to people: that is the story you need to tell.

Research indicates that an inspiring, well-told story can overcome a mound of contradicting statistics. For example, despite statistics that tell of thousands of vacationers who are happy to go to Mexico, my wife will never return after hearing a friend's story about a truly horrible experience. Your resisters know the power of stories, and you can bet they are telling their own horror stories to sow discontent. Therefore, back your information with stories that stir strong, positive emotions and point to a desirable future.

TAKEAWAYS FOR YOUR CHANGE INITIATIVE

- Create a communication cadence.
- Start early — people need time to process and prepare for the change.
- Tackle misinformation directly.
- Teach people how to discriminate among information sources so they can determine which sources are trustworthy and reliable.
- Get creative when communicating — make your messages stand out above the noise.
- Use multiple channels.
- Break the message down into smaller steps if people are feeling overwhelmed.
- Make it personal — appeal to the individual's self-interest — what's in it for them, their families, their communities, and so forth.
- Tell stories that make personal connections.
- Share stories about what happens if people don't adapt.
- Make the change plan clear to foster a sense of control.

STRATEGY 8
ENABLE CHANGE BY REMOVING BARRIERS

WHO KNEW TOILET PAPER would become more valuable than gold? In the span of a day, shelves normally stacked with personal paper goods and cleaning supplies were bare. Queues formed outside stores that went on for blocks. How would the elderly cope? Once they got into a store, would they have to fight off the younger and fitter to get what they needed?

When focused on a goal, it can be difficult to see the obstacles you will encounter along the way. The changes we think seem simple and straightforward are downright threatening to others. It's the reason we must ask ourselves, "What conditions could make this change more difficult for people?" Your speed bump is someone else's impassable mountain.

If the change proves to be excessively painful or damaging, adoption becomes impossible. As change leaders, we have a responsibility to identify those barriers to change and either remove them or help people work through them to arrive at the goal.

THE EVIDENCE

We've already explored the fact that specific stakeholder groups (elderly, isolated, disabled) found the expectations for change (masks, social distancing) challenging to meet even their basic needs (groceries, medical assistance, social stimulation). As the pandemic progressed, additional barriers arose, which governments, nonprofit agencies, and neighbors worked hard to address to enable people to comply with desired change. We saw this most noticeably in strategies that encouraged vaccination.

As the pandemic continued to unfold, an increasing number of barriers came to light. Notice how different enablers removed barriers to promote adaptation to change.

Income Barriers

No work, no income. If I'm worried about finding the next dollar, I will not be focused on embracing change. Individuals and businesses cried out for assistance during lockdown. Unable to work or sell their wares and services, many faced a steep drop in income, compromising their ability to pay the rent or mortgage, let alone buy groceries.

Governments responded by sending cash to citizens and, in many cases, made the criteria very simple to expedite the process. For businesses, the application process was more challenging, but governments made funds available to help them weather lean times.

Airlines struggled under rampant cancellations. Their revenue crashed. Travelers feared losing their airfare money if they tested positive prior to a flight and many chose to fly anyway, knowing they could be contagious. Carriers adapted by suspending change fees so infected passengers could rebook without penalty.

Medical Barriers

How can I live if I'm constantly at threat of being infected? Clearly, some populations required vaccinations more urgently than others. Studying the numbers, ruling bodies prioritized the elderly and the immunocompromised according to their higher risk level. Vaccines were rolled out in a (mostly) orderly manner.

However, for some, the vaccine itself posed a health risk. Unable to safely vaccinate, these individuals needed a pass that would give them access to public places. This took longer to arrange and was fraught with difficulties at the beginning. When mask exemptions became available, governments gave out pass cards too readily, and many people easily copied and distributed their pass cards. This process was so challenging and flawed, Alberta rapidly scrapped its initial approach until it came up with something more secure. In retrospect, government and health leaders could have anticipated and prepared for these medical barriers much earlier in the pandemic.

Social Barriers

Some people need others to look out for them. They lack the social network to get help when help is desperately needed. That's where good neighbors really shine.

During the pandemic, neighbors stepped up, putting out offers on Facebook and other platforms to help community members in need. Need groceries? Need garbage taken out? Just need to talk? There's a neighbor for that (Kitchener.CTVnews.ca).

When businesses struggled to stay afloat, they also began to help each other, promoting the concept of buying local (CBC.ca). One smart barber provided customers with a coupon for the pizza place down the street. Brilliant.

Barriers of Belief

During a change effort, some people need more convincing to embrace change. They may need things explained three or four times before they start to understand or believe them. That's normal. Mainstream media repeated key messages aimed at convincing people to obey the guidelines and get vaccinated.

While the Chinese government ordered compliance, in democratic nations free speech enabled loud arguments in all directions. Beliefs about what was true were subject to the media outlet you tuned into, and — without controls on what people could say (fact, falsehoods, or just plain outrageous) — the confusing messages made it difficult to drive adoption for undecided groups, let alone entrenched anti-vaxxers.

While people were encouraged to return to work, beliefs about contagion created additional barriers. To return to work, employees needed to feel safe. To overcome this barrier, some organizations leveraged a network of change agents, which we first explored in Strategy 4. Dr. Adina Weinerman, the medical director for quality and patient safety at Sunnybrook Health Sciences Centre in Toronto, observed the hesitancy among her fellow healthcare workers and decided to do something to reassure them about the safety of the vaccine (CBC.ca). Her team trained more than 100 colleagues as vaccine champions. These peer advocates made themselves available for a range of team meetings, group huddles, and one-on-one chats to respond to vaccine concerns among staff members without pressure.

At the time of the interview, Sunnybrook had achieved 95 percent vaccination, preventing gaps in service delivery as the organization's mandate deadline approached. The secret? Authenticity and information. Her team's openness and willingness to answer any possible question while defusing falsehoods shifted perception and encouraged adoption.

"I think by opening the conversation with some of the biggest questions we've heard or even some of the things that felt the most outlandish, [this approach] opened it up so that everyone knew there was no question whatsoever that was off limits," she said. "We took as many different approaches as we could to get as many staff trusted, trustworthy information that they could rely on and sort of dispel those myths," said Dr. Weinerman.

Change agents who come from within your stakeholder groups have a massive advantage in swaying others because they are credible as peers. They can empathize and speak the same language. They are influencers.

Privacy Barriers

What if people don't feel they can talk about the impact of change safely? In some places, COVID-positive individuals were shunned. Fear can stop change in its tracks. To overcome that, when someone tested positive in South Korea, a case officer from the local council was assigned to work with them. The case officer initially contacted the person by phone to advise the individuals and family members about isolation procedures. No one showed up at the door where neighbors were watching. Next, the case officer arranged for a stay-at-home kit to be delivered as discreetly as possible to protect the person's privacy. The kit contained essentials, including food, face masks, and sanitizer, to eradicate the need to go out in public. The case officer could customize the kits to include particular foods, medication, or pet care (TheConversation.com).

Language and Access Barriers

Without an understanding of expectations, people cannot adopt change. To understand, we must be speaking the same language. Take note of the importance of overcoming language and access barriers in a success story from my home town. The city of Calgary is divided into quadrants. When vaccination began, officials noted that the northeast quadrant — a lower-income area with a highly diverse population — lagged significantly behind the others. Local leaders identified "many barriers, from work schedules, to shift work, to transportation, to language barriers, to access to technology or Wi-Fi," said Anila Lee Yuen, president and CEO at the Centre for Newcomers (CalgaryHerald.com).

To accommodate these issues, Calgary health and government officials set up multiple clinics in that quadrant. For example, one clinic accommodated appointments for those who needed more control over their schedule, and one focused on walk-ins for those who lacked internet access or weren't savvy with the scheduling system.

The city partnered with several nonprofits: the Centre for Newcomers, Immigrant Services Calgary, and the Mosaic Primary

Care Network. These were all existing, trusted services for the target stakeholder groups. Working together, they distributed critical information about vaccination to those who needed it. The city translated vaccination posters into seventy-two languages and distributed them throughout the community. International medical graduates were on-site to answer questions in a variety of languages.

In November 2021, the city celebrated a 99 percent first-vaccination rate for the northeast quadrant, surpassing every other quadrant. "I'm ecstatic that all the hard work that we've put in, all of the advocacy and all of the resources that went into the community actually had this kind of a profound effect. We're literally as a community able to save lives by putting all those resources there," said Lee Yuen. "Really, the secret sauce, the silver bullet in terms of why this works is we met the need for the community, and we did that through respect and collaboration for the community and each other."

REMOVE BARRIERS: THE ANALYSIS

Score: D

Why such a low score based on the evidence? It's because of timing and agency.

When your stakeholders include literally everyone on the planet, it's difficult to anticipate all possible barriers to change, but government and health leaders could have easily predicted a variety of major barriers and proactively planned ways to avoid or overcome them. Some barriers were only recognized once they evolved into major pain points that stirred a huge outcry from everyday citizens. For example, leaders tackled vaccine barriers only as vaccination rates slowed. That's too late and reflects tunnel vision on the part of leaders.

In many cases, agents outside of government stepped in to overcome barriers: volunteers, nonprofits, and neighbors, with the vast majority acting independently rather than waiting for the government to bless their efforts. As mentioned earlier, a friend in Los Angeles used personal contacts to move personal protective gear directly from a manufacturer to a hospital in need, a situation that repeated itself around the world. Official channels were not getting it done.

While COVID-19 Rescue Plan payments and unemployment benefits were welcomed by all, they continued for too long. And as the economy ramped up, many employees felt no inclination to return to work when the government was paying them to do absolutely nothing. Removing one barrier created a new one.

These misses created a final barrier to embracing change: trust. When the organization's response is bungled and inadequate, trust is eroded. No trust, no adoption. This was certainly the case in the US where trust in federal institutions has been declining for years.

When the leaders of change cannot be trusted, we need the intervention of those we do trust — those with whom we have strong relationships: influencers. That's why peer change agents are so important. They operate locally. They look us in the eye and let us know their first priority is to help. They have our best interests in mind. Engaging them proactively to help identify and resolve barriers is a critical best practice for leaders of change.

Consider Puerto Rico, which had endured poor government support during past crises, particularly after the hurricane of 2017 and earthquake of 2019. Non-governmental organizations (NGOs) had picked up the slack to deliver needed care where overwhelmed government institutions could not. When the pandemic struck, "government officials, scientists, physicians, pharmacists, the National Guard, and religious and community leaders rallied in a unified campaign around the vaccine and COVID-19 prevention" (Vox.com). NGOs and community members once again stepped in to fill the gap to deliver information and services, utilizing the relationships developed during past crises. They successfully overcame barriers because they had developed trust.

LESSONS FOR CHANGE LEADERS

While strong and credible leadership is critical to inspire change, practical interventions are just as important to enable people to adapt. We must make it easy for people to comply. With each barrier they encounter, the risk they will give up on the goal increases. Identifying and removing barriers is an essential part of leading effective programs of change.

First, take time to identify barriers. Ask representatives from all your stakeholder groups, "What could get in the way of adopting this change? What could make it easier or more difficult?" Consider the actual conditions under which people will need to apply the change. Here are a few prompts:

- While mobile
- In remote locations (with weak or absent internet access)
- In poor weather or extremes of hot and cold
- At night
- When tired or under pressure
- In front of customers or in socially sensitive situations
- In other languages or within different cultures

Will your stakeholders be able to meet your expectations in each situation? Review the common barriers discussed in this strategy and outlined in the takeaway list below. Note that I've added some additional barriers that were not apparent in the pandemic but are highly relevant in most change situations, particularly the lack of critical knowledge or a specific skill.

New behaviors often require new learning. This is most commonly remedied through training, but that is rarely sufficient. Wise change leaders ask, "What is the level of competency that people need to achieve?" If we want sales and service reps to stand in front of customers and deliver exactly the right approach after they are trained on the change, we are likely to be disappointed. Interaction, job shadowing, role playing, and coaching beyond the classroom are all necessary to help people achieve a high level of confidence and competence to perform new skills and exhibit new behaviors. Managers play a critical role in the process of building and reinforcing new behaviors. They must be well equipped to carry out their role as supporting leaders in the change.

As a first step, carefully examine your message. You might think issues of language don't apply in the business world. They do. I guarantee that you and your team will have developed a lingo around the details of the disruption. Reading unfamiliar terms and acronyms is a turnoff for any audience. Make it simple, avoid jargon, and test drive your messages with people outside of the project. If they cannot understand your message, they cannot comply.

Second, identify your enablers and influencers who could operate as change agents to help people get past the barriers. Who is in a position to help you achieve success? Don't limit yourself to those in authority. Review your stakeholder assessment and consider those with influence and relationships in your organization. Who do people look up to? Who always seems to get consulted? Who is willing to lend a hand when people get stuck?

Third, work together with your change agents to remove barriers. Use discussions, demonstrations, and offers of personal and practical assistance to help your stakeholders see that there is a clear path to success during disruption.

Give your change agents open access to your team to ask questions and receive fast support. This will enable them to quickly deliver the level of assistance required at the front line of change. Plus, it will keep them energized about the change process and the end goal. (You do not want change agents to become frustrated and disillusioned.) Keep them supplied with a constant flow of useful information they can share. Give them tools for success, such as dedicated chat channels and access to real-time reports.

When your change agents identify new barriers, provide the time and attention needed to help them overcome those barriers. Endorse them publicly as ambassadors if needed (but not if your endorsement will lessen their credibility) to give them the authority to help others. Keep them motivated, and get out of their way.

One more best practice requires particular mention. In the strategy about communication, we looked at the power of stories. Sharing stories of success helps people envision themselves as successful, too. However, sharing stories of failure can have a similarly positive effect. We need people to feel safe enough to reveal when they are struggling or making errors along the path of change. Covering up challenges, hurdles, and mistakes can lead to much greater headaches.

Therefore, sharing stories of failures without shaming anyone — while emphasizing why these mistakes are normal and to be expected and how people resolved them — is a critical tool to empower people to take those first, uncomfortable steps toward embracing change.

Here's an example: "John was one of our first people to try the new system. His first entry had fourteen errors, and that's OK. We caught it in our daily report, and, by his second day, he was 100 percent error free! Mistakes will happen. We want you to try. Our change team is ready to help you whenever you need it."

Every change comes with obstacles to success. Proactively identifying and removing obstacles at the outset of the change initiative — and then quickly addressing new barriers that emerge — is the key to keeping people moving toward the goal. Show them you have a plan for the most challenging scenarios. When resistance sets in, rely on those closest to your stakeholders to help them get through the challenges and experience success.

TAKEAWAYS FOR YOUR CHANGE INITIATIVE

- Consider barriers of:
  - Income
  - Language
  - Social networks
  - Technology
  - Transportation and geography
  - Skills
  - Privacy
  - Beliefs
  - Access
- Consider credibility: Do stakeholders have reason to distrust leaders of the change? Is it better if direction comes from someone else?
- Identify and tackle barriers proactively:
  - For each group, what could get in the way of adoption?
  - Identify change agents who have influence over and trusted relationships with the stakeholders.
  - Enable change agents to help you begin removing obstacles proactively and as they emerge.
- Share stories of success and stories of failure to motivate and promote open sharing of struggles. This provides evidence that the change project is moving forward, and the end goal is in sight.

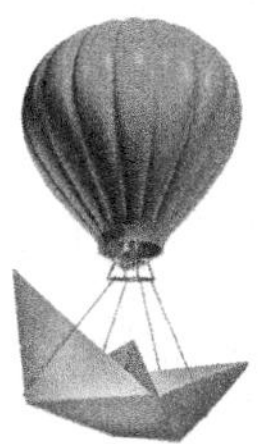

STRATEGY 9 RESPOND TO RESISTANCE: WHEN COERCION IS THE BEST OPTION

"I WILL NOT EAT MY PEAS!" Every parent recognizes the face of resistance: arms crossed, huge frown, lower lip extended. The expression remains quite similar into adulthood. Sometimes people just will not get on board, and no amount of dialogue or outright begging is going to change that. In fact, it will likely make it worse.

Resistance occurs on a continuum. While some people readily comply and commit to changes, others struggle. They want to change but need more help. Sometimes the issue is with barriers as we saw in the last strategy. Others are entrenched in their opposing position. They will do everything possible to avoid making the change. They look for workarounds that undermine the change. When barriers show up, they are the first to quit in their attempts to adopt the change. This strategy was written for those situations.

THE EVIDENCE

When vaccines were approved, people rejoiced around the world! Vaccination rates took off for those who had access to them. And then those rates slowed and, in many cases, stalled. Now what? After conversations and convincing and removal of barriers, government leaders had a few more levers to apply. They could promote incentives, communicate consequences of noncompliance, issue mandates, and enforce those mandates. Let's take a closer look at these four responses to resistance.

Incentivize Stakeholders

Why not offer cash? Several governments ran lotteries. Minnesota offered $25 Visa gift cards, fishing licenses, state park passes, and tickets to the state fair. These incentives certainly moved some folks to get vaccinated, but the consensus was that they had minimal impact. It also had a negative impact on the uptake for future vaccinations.

Highlight Consequences of Noncompliance

Every pack of cigarettes in North America includes scary pictures of the many ways smoking will make my life (and others) miserable. For COVID-19, we were regularly reminded of the consequences of not complying — if you get infected, you may die. Or you may pass it on to a family member who may die. Children could grow up without their grandparents, or worse, without their parents.

These sound like strong deterrents to noncompliance. Were they? Given the situation — a pandemic with a runaway deadly virus — highlighting these dramatic consequences to noncompliance was appropriate.

Issue Mandates

If they won't comply, they can be made to comply. Governments mandated that all public servants be vaccinated or lose their jobs. Hospitals and nursing homes adopted mandates to protect the workforce and the patients. Big corporations got on board as well.

Mandates absolutely drove higher adoption rates for vaccination. Mandates made the need for change very real and very personal. Loss of job meant loss of income and loss of the freedom that money provides.

Enforce the Mandates

Coercion doesn't work if there is no threat behind the mandate. Much of the enforcement during the pandemic came from peers rather than authority: The retail clerks at the doors reminding you to put on your mask and sanitize. Fellow shoppers nudging people to put their masks over their noses. Some businesses doled out fines for noncompliance.

The reality in Canada was that it was relatively easy for many people to flout the rules because typical citizens would rather avoid conflict when peers refused to comply. For example, it was unreasonable to expect part-time students working at a store to stand up to shoppers who did not have a mask. And fines to businesses were inconsistently applied.

Several institutions faced with the loss of a significant number of staff members allowed mandate deadlines to slip. They simply could not afford to draw a hard line. Police unions threatened walkouts in the face of mandates and did not respond to most complaints of violations. Several states in the US presented legal cases against the use of corporate mandates for vaccination. Other states moved to limit the ability of health leaders to impose restrictions, undermining their authority over public safety. Unless you were attempting to board a plane, mandates in many organizations had no teeth.

RESPOND TO RESISTANCE: THE ANALYSIS

Score: C

"If it is so safe, why are you bribing us to take the vaccine?" Incentives are risky. They can send mixed messages and even backfire. In the case of the pandemic, the use of incentives was a failure. In fact, one study found that incentives decreased vaccination rates: "For individuals ages 40 and over, 30-day vaccination rates declined by 4.5 and 4.7 percentage points in response to the $10 and $50 incentives, respectively" (VoxEU.org).

Incentives set a precedent for future compliance. If you were incentivized to get vaccinated, what will it take to motivate you to get a booster? Some countries did, in fact, offer booster bonuses, but it's a never-ending wheel. Token economies do not work. They result in a population of people who will only do what they are paid to do and who may decide at any time that it's no longer worth it.

As for consequences of noncompliance, scare tactics only work when the threat is immediate and highly probable. The monster must be right on your heels to keep you running. That hasn't been the case with COVID-19: many get infected, some get very sick, and a small percentage will die. If you haven't seen that up close, you just might skip the vaccination and take the chance that you can dodge the bullet.

Back to our smokers — they seem quite unaffected by warning labels. They are driven by something else. They want to retain the right to choose, even if the science says it's a bad decision. Similarly, anti-vaxxers resist because they fear something worse from the vaccine itself, whether it be tiny chips and trackers, blood clots, brain-wasting side effects, or simply the loss of freedom of choice. It is extremely difficult to overcome fear. Coercion typically makes it worse; people entrench themselves in their position when facing the use of force.

During the pandemic, mandates were successful where enforced and supported by consistent communication and encouragement. Led by the scientific community, mandates in Puerto Rico drove very high vaccination rates. By contrast, where American police forces pushed back on mandates, adoption was lower in those metropolitan police forces. Since it's far better if people make their own choice to comply, mandates should always be a last resort — and enforced. In the case of COVID-19, leaders could have had more success if they introduced mandates as soon as vaccination rates dropped while sustaining constant affirming communication.

It's important to note that when vaccination became a political agenda item it immediately polarized people, particularly in the United States. Compliance was seen as support for the ruling party, whether you voted for that party or not. Polarization serves as a reminder of the importance of leader credibility when promoting change. Leaders must be able to appeal to all stakeholders, not just the ones who voted for them.

LESSONS FOR CHANGE LEADERS

The best adoption happens when people choose it of their own free will, driven by their own internal motivation. They must believe it is the right thing for them to do. That personal decision reinforces a sense of control and ownership. That's comforting for people. That's also why clear communication and education (give them the facts) are so important when leading change — so people can choose for themselves.

When you encounter resistance, the first step is always to diagnose and determine the reason for resistance. Often it's due to bad information and is rectified easily through communication. Others may be fearful of the change; remind them of the reasons for change and the benefit it has for people (family, friends, customers, and community). Keep their struggles private lest they be ostracized.

If you're considering the use of incentives, consider that it risks making action dependent on something external to the individual: "I'm complying because you are giving me something." This can effectively reduce commitment to the required change. If people do not value the incentive, they will not comply at all. They will hold out for a bigger or different incentive.

Therefore, use small, fun incentives. Stickers, badges, and pins work well. Make it easy for people to earn them. When prizes are inexpensive, psychology tells us that people do not typically ascribe their compliance to the earning of rewards. They are too small to justify the effort, which in turn leads them to conclude that they actually wanted to participate in the change. It was their choice.

Remember our "Difficulty versus Desirability" two-by-two matrix (Figure 3.4)? In the bottom half, we have changes with low desirability — there is little to attract stakeholders to the change. These types of changes are becoming more common as organizations make rapid decisions necessary to compete and survive. The change is disruptive and will present many growing pains. In these situations, coercing change may be the only option to ensure the continued viability of the organization.

Mandates should always be a last resort, used only when nothing else works. People who are forced to comply drag their feet, spread negativity and misinformation, and do the minimum required to satisfy requirements. That is why, even if a mandate becomes necessary, we never stop applying all the other change tactics to encourage people to make their own positive decisions about adapting to the circumstances.

Regardless of superhuman encouragement, removal of barriers, and mandates backed by the power of God, some people in your organization will resist. They will use every excuse available to avoid compliance. If you do not address their resistance, your lack of action will be seen as endorsement. When one person refuses to move and gets away with it, this draws attention. All of a sudden, a whole group of people gets suspicious: "Do we really need to change at all?" Consequences must be clear and enforced. Managers must be equipped to have tough conversations and take action with employees who choose to drag their feet.

Stern conversations don't always convert our resisters. I've worked on many projects where, despite the best use of change tactics, some people would not move. My advice to their leaders? Tell them to either get in line or find a home elsewhere. It seems extreme, but when organizations are focused on a sound strategy for success, they need to move with speed. A bit of bad yeast can spoil the whole batch. Don't take the chance that resistance will spread. Making an example of one person sends a clear message that you are serious about the change and reaching the end goal.

The best approach to minimize resistance and inspire change is to apply all the tactics we've discussed and keep applying them continuously. Even when risk of harm is imminent and failing to comply creates terrible risk for everyone, we prefer that people make decisions of their own volition. When stakeholders choose change on their own terms, this leads to the highest levels of adoption, whether it's getting vaccinated or using a new expense process at work.

Only when changes require immediate action and people are not moving should you consider coercion as the last but necessary option.

TAKEAWAYS FOR YOUR CHANGE INITIATIVE

- We want people to choose to change of their own volition.
- When encountering resistance, first understand the reason for resistance.
- Avoid using manipulation or scare tactics — this only works if the consequences of noncompliance are immediate and highly threatening.
- Incentives can backfire — use them carefully to reinforce your stakeholders' own decision-making process.
- Enforce your decisions. If people can choose noncompliance or work around the change with no consequences, adoption will be low.
- Use coercion as a last resort to push people in the right direction. Make sure you have removed all practical barriers first!
- Never stop sharing information, highlighting benefits, and telling stories of success. Use all the change tactics to continuously encourage adoption.

STRATEGY 10
MEASURE SUCCESS: ARE WE THERE YET?

AT THE CLOSE OF 2022, the World Health Organization provided an official count of 5.5 million deaths from COVID-19 but added that a true estimate would be closer to 15 million. Those are horrific numbers; however, consensus is that it could have been much worse.

Change leaders began the pandemic journey with the end goal in mind: saving lives. It was a tall order when a deadly virus with no known cure disrupted every routine. It was also a long-term goal with no set deadline. No one knew how long lockdowns would last or when a vaccine might become available. The strategic goal was the right one. The tactics — our three rules of masks, sanitizing, and distancing — focused on short-term behavior changes to slow the spread in service of the goal.

When people are asked to radically change the way they live, they want to know if it's working. Worldwide protests showed that some people were not convinced that the rules had any effect at all. There's no point in sustaining such difficult changes, they reasoned, if they don't make a difference. Enter the statisticians.

THE EVIDENCE

During this particular disruption — the COVID-19 pandemic — government and health leaders (as well as millions of citizens around the globe) measured success based on two major criteria: saving lives and saving businesses. Did we make it? Let's take a look.

Saving Lives

"We must flatten the curve." This was an early mantra to motivate compliance with safety measures. If cases surged, the number of hospitalizations would rapidly exceed available capacity. Long lineups at clinics and hospitals dominated the news as worst-case scenarios came to life before our eyes. Intensive care units (ICUs) were maxed out, and respirators were in high demand. We quickly exceeded medical capacity, and the war had just begun.

Government and health leaders began presenting graphs to show us the disastrous effects if we did not comply with the basic rules of masking, sanitizing, and distancing (see Figure 10.1).

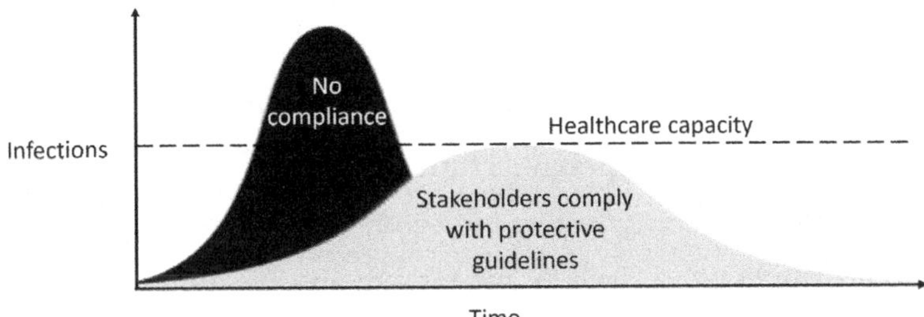

Figure 10.1 This type of diagram, used early in the pandemic, showed how lack of compliance would lead to increased infections, which would exceed the capacity to cope with rising infection rates. During a change initiative, it can be useful to show what will happen if people do not comply with the change.

Success does not look like people waiting outside in the freezing cold to receive help. So, how did we know if we were moving in the right direction? How did we know if protective measures were actually flattening the curve, while we experienced the immediate pain of adopting entirely new behaviors to conform to difficult new practices? We needed data.

Every day we scanned the news for a handful of numbers: new cases, test positivity rate, hospitalizations, and deaths. These were lagging indicators, telling us after the fact whether we were getting the virus under control.

Ironically, the number of deaths was the best indicator of success, and it indicated failure. Too many people died, particularly among our seniors. In the initial surge, we failed to flatten the curve, and many deaths were due to an overloaded healthcare system that could not isolate or treat so many infected patients. Plus, we know that some people did not go to the healthcare system for help because they feared picking up something worse in that environment.

Lagging indicators were helpful, but we needed leading indicators that could predict potential future issues and eventual success. During the pandemic, leading indicators came in the form of news about compliance as well as violent and abusive noncompliance, which demonstrated a mixed bag of success. Would the resisters neutralize everyone else's efforts?

Conformance levels did predict drops in cases and deaths. Isolation reduced infection rates. Conversely, loosening restrictions drove increases in cases. Measurements helped us understand the virus trajectory.

As vaccines became available, the vaccination rate became the most important leading indicator of success. With vaccines dramatically cutting the probability of severe illness and death, they were our best defense for saving lives in the long run. Starting in the fall of 2021, government and health leaders further expanded vaccine rate reporting with details about the percentages of first, second, and third vaccination doses.

Beyond compliance and physical health measurements, surveys gave us data about the flipside of our physical lives: our mental health. Around the world, mental health took a major hit from forced isolation, constant fear, grief for those who lost loved ones, and the energy drain of being mindful of masks, sanitizing, and distancing. Change added a significant layer of stress for many people by complicating routine tasks and putting a stranglehold on our ability to socialize. Even if people survived the virus, would they be broken?

LifeWorks maintained a monthly Mental Health Index, comparing it to pre-pandemic levels (LifeWorks.com). Unsurprisingly, scores dropped as signs of distress increased. Instances of the word burnout in the news and employee conversations rose dramatically. Mental health indicators told us that it's possible we may have won the battle with COVID-19 while losing the war to save lives based on emotional scars from the pandemic years. Time will tell.

Saving Businesses

Overall, businesses fared well because of the massive government cash outlays, bridging the gap until restrictions could be eased. But survival wasn't the only measure.

JUST Capital tracked American opinions through the pandemic (JUSTcapital.com):

- Nine in ten Americans agreed it was an opportunity for large companies to hit "reset" and focus on doing right by their stakeholders.
- Eighty percent said the pandemic had "opened my eyes to acceptable and unacceptable corporate behavior."
- Eighty-four percent agreed that "I will remember the companies that did the right thing by their workers by ensuring their health and safety or doing their best to avoid layoffs."

Doing the right thing means making tough decisions to do what's right in the eyes of employees versus shareholders. Many organizations took the opportunity to help employees and members of their community, investing profits into lives. The public took notice, and these stats help us predict future organizational success. When employees and customers lose faith in organizations, both performance and sales drop. Doing what's right is a critical measurement of our true commitment to purpose, and that's what inspires action.

MEASURE SUCCESS: THE ANALYSIS

Score: B

In April 2021, India surpassed 350,000 daily cases of COVID-19. December 2021 saw the UK reporting more than 100,000 cases in a day. Those were scary numbers. Depressing. They told a story of pain for millions of people experiencing the anxiety of tests, waiting for results, isolation, fear, loss, and grief.

But cases and deaths were the right measurements to keep people informed about both the seriousness of the virus and the importance of continued vigilance as we fought it. These lagging indicators remain the ultimate measurements of success. In addition, the leading indicators concerning compliance and vaccination rates were equally important in predicting infection rates and eventual success.

However, leaders missed opportunities to use data better. In terms of the final goal of saving lives, the death count would have been better balanced if they also had presented the discharge rate as a measurement of success. Yes, people were getting infected and winding up in ICU, but the vast majority were being discharged after effective treatment. Lives were being saved.

The "flatten the curve" graphic was an important and powerful visual to motivate behavior change, but we never did see what the actual curve looked like. Leaders could have used it more effectively to communicate success by superimposing actual infection rates over hospital capacity or respirator availability.

Images and statistics can help tell your story in a change initiative so give careful thought to how they can powerfully communicate information to help you motivate change.

This brings us to another important measurement to motivate people. Long COVID arose as a real concern. How long could symptoms last? Would it leave you with brain fog, fatigue, and respiratory issues for years? Doctors and research scientists are still addressing these questions. Even as vaccines continue to dampen the infection rate in this post-pandemic era, seeing stats for long COVID would help remind people to continue to comply with basic safety measures to avoid getting infected at all. We need better numbers in this area.

Beware Segmentation

In the United States, vaccination rates were compared along political lines. Calling out unique groups (segments) is a double-edged sword. On the one hand, it can show us where we need to employ extra or different strategies to achieve change. It can also spark healthy competition. But on the other hand, it can contribute to racism, ageism, and every other form of negative discrimination. We saw it all during the pandemic.

In my home province of Alberta, our two biggest cities of Calgary and Edmonton both have professional hockey and football teams, which has traditionally driven a certain level of friendly rivalry. The reporting of COVID-19 measurements by city elevated that rivalry to hate, in some cases. It enabled finger-pointing rather than healthy competition.

When government and health agencies rolled out vaccines, hospitalization rates were split to indicate the percentage of admitted patients who were vaccinated. While this was rightfully intended to inspire people to get the jab, it also decreased tolerance. Some argued that stubborn anti-vaxxers who got sick and were admitted to hospitals were sucking up important healthcare resources, thereby preventing vaccinated people from getting the critical surgeries they had been waiting for. Their choice to avoid the jab drove the extension of restrictions, preventing many others from attending family events to receive badly needed hugs. Change leaders need to carefully handle segmentation of data.

Did you notice an interesting turn in the domain of measurements? As people pushed to get their lives back, a new set of measurements emerged to indicate success in battling COVID-19:

- Volume of airline flights and travelers
- Sales of party dresses
- Gym membership renewals
- Number of live events
- Zoom's share price falling
- Helpful measurements can come from many places.

LESSONS FOR CHANGE LEADERS

When the change is fully in place, when people have adopted it, what does that future look like, feel like, and even smell like? When we have reached our end goal, what are people doing and saying? These questions provide important clues for the measurements we need to track. From customer surveys to cycle-time measurements, we need baselines and progress reports to tell us where we need to adjust our strategy.

Starting with the end in mind includes determining what indicates success. While this strategy comes near the end of the book, the work begins during Strategy 1. When we ask the change leadership team to clarify the goal, they should be able to paint the picture of the future with specificity. If we know what we want people to do differently, we can begin to measure it.

Measurement is rarely that simple. The data we require may not exist. Or the specifics of the goal are still being worked out. "Do we need a ninety percent adoption rate or ninety-five? Should all customers notice the difference in our service levels or just a majority? What is an appropriate error rate when employees use the new system during the first six months?" The key for you is to not give up on asking questions and clarifying specific answers so you can devise useful measurements and begin tracking the data.

As you share progress with your stakeholders along the way, keep in mind that your audience can get lost in the numbers and lose sight of the larger goal. Consider that, during the pandemic, learning about thousands of deaths per day became the norm. Later, we barely felt the reality of a few hundred deaths per day when it was thousands not long ago. Numbers get stale unless we surround them with meaning. That's why you must back up data by telling the story of change.

Success is not a number. It is a journey marked by sacrifices and triumphs, failures and eventual success. Those are the stories you tell again and again to remind people of the reality of change — the good and the bad.

As you determine the scope and target for your change program, identify the leading and lagging measurements that define success. Establishing baselines early will help you tell the entire story.

TAKEAWAYS FOR YOUR CHANGE INITIATIVE

- Ask, "What does success look like?"
- Keep pressing for the details so you can establish baselines.
- Identify measurements that indicate success.
- Include early, ongoing, and final measurements.
- Use both leading and lagging measurements.
- Embed data in stories that help your stakeholders understand the importance of the numbers.

STRATEGY 11
SUSTAIN SUCCESS: DOUBLING DOWN ON CHANGE

WE SENT MY SON TO THE BASEMENT. On New Year's Eve, he tested positive after attending a party, so he paid the price with isolation. It's a decent gig being locked up with a big-screen TV, full VR rig, and a mini fridge with regular meal delivery from the parents. Sheesh. Was this really necessary?

I admit that I became numb to the virus. I grew tired of the surface wipe-downs and constantly being mindful of everything I touched. Wash, wipe, and sanitize. Ugh. Physically it wasn't a problem, but mentally I got exhausted with the whole routine.

The truth is that I feared the dentist more than I feared COVID-19, and that made change hard to sustain, even before initial vaccination doses and regular boosters became a reality. But I soldiered on because of the risk to those I love and care about.

Even for the most successful change, we need to recognize the risk that, over time, people will return to previous ways of behaving. The probability of relapse increases as change becomes more difficult. How do we sustain new behavior?

In the simplest terms, sustainment requires change leaders to continue to use all the best change tactics we've been applying throughout the entire transformation. We continuously remind people about what to do, reward them for adaptive behaviors, and tell stories of success.

THE EVIDENCE

Throughout the pandemic, we saw the entire range of responses, from people lining up for hours to get the vaccine to disrespectful and sometimes dangerous protests at hospitals and ceremonies honoring our war veterans (CBC.ca). Sustaining new behaviors throughout the pandemic was not easy. Let's explore each tactic change leaders used to keep people on course.

Remind

Every shop you entered had reminders about masks, sanitizing, and distancing. The news repeated this message, our leaders emphasized it, and it was broadcast over speaker systems as we shopped. Each day we read the numbers. "Are cases up or down?" ICU and death rates reminded us of the potential consequences of noncompliance.

Government and health leaders vigorously promoted vaccines. Many people reinforced this through social media as they posted selfies and proudly wore stickers after getting the jab. To assist with reinforcement, leaders repeated key messages and risks and benefits through the cycle of first, second, and third doses.

Reward

If you read the news, the numbers indicated the rewards of diligence. In countries like South Korea and New Zealand compliance clearly led to low case and death rates. The reward was a low risk of infection.

Then there were more direct incentives as we saw in Strategy 9. Many governments offered cash and other rewards for vaccination. But money doesn't motivate for very long. It cannot sustain behavior over time without continuous and increasing incentives. However, the ability to return to work and earn money is an excellent motivator. It allows people to act with purpose again and find fulfilment in carrying out tasks that benefit themselves and others.

I was pleased to observe so many handmade signs and acts of generosity toward our healthcare heroes during the pandemic. Working with daily exposure to a deadly virus is draining work, and they needed our encouragement. As the spouse of a healthcare worker, I can tell you that supportive horn-honking and restaurant discounts were welcome rewards for enduring the daily donning of personal protective equipment. It gets hot in there!

With the wide adoption of vaccine passports, those who complied were rewarded with the ability to travel and eat in restaurants. Romantic dates could go beyond Zoom calls. The rewards of obedience became tangible. Vaccination spelled freedom for many. For those who chose not to comply, career options narrowed in the face of mandates and revised job descriptions that required vaccination.

Tell Stories

Yes, here it is again. Witnessing suffering up close and personal is often an inspiration for change. Storytelling achieves the same effect by helping others connect with the lives of strangers to relate and learn from their experiences.

Every day, we could read stories of those struggling in ICU, the survivors, and those still suffering the effects of long COVID. These stories were often hard to read, but their weight was a strong force to convince others to keep in compliance.

On the positive side, I made a point of asking my clients, "How old do you think is the oldest person to have pulled through COVID-19?" No one guessed correctly. The answer: Cornelia Ras of the Netherlands at 107 years of age. "We did not expect her to survive this," said her niece Maaike de Groot. "She takes no medicines, still walks well and gets down on her knees every night to thank the Lord. From the looks of it, she will be able to continue to do so." Wow!

Stories offer us critical hope during difficult change, motivate us to adapt, and help us sustain our new behaviors.

SUSTAIN SUCCESS: THE ANALYSIS

Score: A

The fight against COVID-19 rarely took a break, with cities, states, provinces, and nations bouncing back and forth between restoring a sense of normality and reverting to harsh lockdown rules as new variants emerged. The consequent whiplash was extremely difficult — even depressing — to endure. However, as the pattern repeated, it did serve to reinforce the basic behaviors required for safety.

The problem? The constant shifting of safety rules as we learned more and as COVID-19 cases raged and receded resulted in confusion and exhaustion. From one day to the next, people were unsure which rules were in place. Some governments locked down hard at the first sniff of a resurgence, while others waited until cases were peaking before reinstituting measures. International travelers had even more challenges navigating rules as they moved between nations. Inconsistency and confusion reigned.

But there was a silver lining to all the confusion. At some point, it became easier to just maintain the basics — mask, sanitize, and distance — regardless of what was going on. Two years into the pandemic, wearing a mask was no longer an issue of comfort. It was status quo. And honestly, I prefer to sanitize frequently these days, even without the looming threat of COVID-19. This is reinforcement to the max.

Booster shots are an important physical reminder that the virus is still with us. Regular boosters have created a rhythm of vaccination. Once is not enough. Governments are now recommending a booster every year, folding it into the regular cadence of flu shots. Doing so normalizes the change and embeds it in our annual cycle of activities. This is good: people love predictable rhythms and, for change to truly take hold, it must become part of the way we live.

I have one final word of advice regarding the challenge of maintaining our commitment to change. Over time, we tune out static messages. We don't see the signs anymore. Repeated store announcements become background noise. We lose sight of the risk. Government and health leaders will continually be challenged with finding new ways to send the message and break through our short attention spans. That's why storytelling will continue to be important as a powerful reminder to remain vigilant. From person to person, the story is never the same. New stories keep the message fresh.

LESSONS FOR CHANGE LEADERS

Our goal is to have people adopt new behaviors to achieve a specific end goal. All the tactics in this book are used to that end. When can we stop applying them? To answer that, we need to understand how people interpret and respond to change over time.

When leaders advocate change, some people are immediately turned off at the notion of being told what to do. They resist. If messages come from a powerful or respected source and are backed with rewards and consequences, a portion of the audience will comply using the reasoning that, "I'm doing it because I have to." As people become educated with more information and come to understand what's in it for them and the people they care about, some will upgrade from compliance to commitment; they have made a personal decision to buy in. Figure 11.1 shows the progression from defiance to compliance to commitment to conviction.

If the consequences of noncompliance are particularly daunting or the call for compliance is inspiring, some stakeholders will become convicted at a deeper level of the need for change. This position spawns advocates or agents of change, people who will spread the message and work to influence others to decide in favor of the change as well. This is the best possible outcome. For large, complex change, a single leader cannot do it alone.

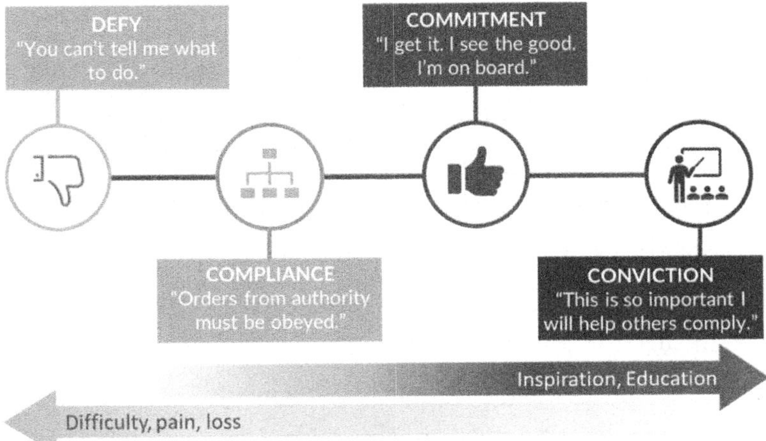

Figure 11.1 Adopting a change requires each person to commit to that change, However, the commitment level is on a continuum and can change over time according to several factors.

But these states of defiance, compliance, commitment, and conviction are not static. We are always learning by observation and taking in new information. People can be persuaded away from defiance, but, likewise, those on board may choose to resist over time. Just as inspiration and education act to motivate people to buy in, frustration, disillusionment, and pain become forces that push people back toward defiance.

What does this all mean? The job is not over. Clearly, some tactics no longer make sense once we get the majority of our stakeholders moving in the desired direction, but we need to be aware of the risk that some people will regress. Once the change has been instituted, we can then consider what to stop, start, and continue.

Stop . . .

Remove all references to the old way of working. If you developed training to move people from the previous state to the new state, it is likely time to end the transition training or update it so it reflects the new current state, post-change.

Now is the time to remove anything that would permit people to go back to previous ways of behaving. That might include uninstalling software, removing links, or recycling old forms and instructions.

Ensure the performance management system reflects new expectations. That might include revising job descriptions accordingly. These elements are commonly missed and can lead to confusion when existing systems seem to reward old ways of working. Don't forget this important detail!

Start . . .

When change becomes the norm, this often impacts the onboarding process. What do you want every new hire to know about this change so they are prepared to behave in agreement with what you've accomplished. Consider whether they need to be advised that you are still working through some resistance issues. The worst thing that can happen is for new hires to be unduly influenced by a rebel faction in the organization.

Update your measurements, if needed. When you are past the transition date, it may be time to shift to new data, such as customer feedback or supplier delivery time.

Begin transitioning activities that are handled by the soon-to-be-dissolved project team over to the business. You may need to designate new leaders, owners, or caretakers as points of contact for process changes, questions, system and data management, and training. Ensure you have clean hand-off discussions.

Continue . . .

Communication! Your newsletter format may change, but don't stop communicating successes and failures. The frequency will decrease over time as the change becomes the norm, but your change-related communication needs to extend at least two months past the transition point. Sometimes it needs to continue much longer if the change is difficult and you need to continuously reinforce new behaviors.

Throughout the process, remind your stakeholders about the goal, what everyone has achieved so far, and what still remains to be done. Be honest about problems that have occurred and what people need to know to avoid them. Give them lead times for fixes that are in progress. These elements provide a sense of order during what may seem like an ongoing, chaotic transition.

If you are rolling out or responding to a highly disruptive change, I strongly encourage you to run weekly, if not daily, live meetings to update your leaders and influencers. Once the change has begun, I run sessions for a combination of managers and change agents so we can freely exchange what is working, what's broken, and how people are reacting. We review data and listen to stories from the front line. This is critical information to adapt your plan on the fly. I constantly receive positive feedback from these meetings; people feel respected when change leaders are there to listen and respond. I ramp up these sessions a couple of weeks prior to launch and continue to hold them as long as they prove valuable while people are adapting.

At this point in the book, you know that storytelling is an excellent method to encourage high levels of commitment to the change. Don't stop now! Stories convert cold facts into real people just like you and me. When stories enable us to see ourselves in those who succeed and fail (then succeed), we are more likely to believe we are able to adapt to the change. Stories that demonstrate hope (107-year-old woman survives COVID!) are often the most effective at inspiring action.

The power of stories reminds us of one more important secret of success for change leaders: they hunt down new stories relentlessly. People get tired of hearing the same story about Jonathan's success over and over. Mix it up. Ask your people why they embraced the change and how they succeeded. Find out how people who failed were able to get back on track. What did they learn? Ask how people in different stakeholder groups adopted the change. Get stories from a wide variety of individuals, such as frontline customer support personnel, field workers in various regions or countries, and those who are technical as well as those who are not.

Continue to uncover and share new stories — by text and video — and use them to continually inspire your audience with the message that failure is normal, success is possible, and they can overcome any barrier. Give your people hope!

TAKEAWAYS FOR YOUR CHANGE INITIATIVE

- Left unchecked, changes are at risk if people revert to previous behaviors.
- Sustainment requires repeating all the tactics used to successfully inspire change.
- Stop delivering transition training for the change initiative. Stop using outdated procedure manuals, performance tools, and job descriptions. Update them as needed.
- Start updating your onboarding training and the measurements you are tracking. Begin transitioning tasks that are handled by the change project team to the business.
- Continue to:
    - Remind stakeholders of the who, what, why, when, where, and how of change.
    - Acknowledge the difficulty of sustaining change and continue to encourage compliance.
    - Ask a wide variety of stakeholders how they succeeded or recovered from failure.
    - Inspire hope by continually sharing new stories about success, how people were able to turn around failures, and what they learned along the way to adopting change.

STRATEGY 12
WRAP IT UP: CLOSING MEANS CLEANING UP

MY MOTHER WAS WRONG. Now, before you send me a note to see if I survived the aftermath of her disappointment when she read this strategy, let me explain. Mom always said, "Leave things the way you found them." That's about respect, and when I'm using other people's stuff, I do my best to honor her words. It's good advice.

But when it comes to change, we never leave things the way we found them. That would be failure. Our purpose is to lead the disruption toward something better.

Everyone is relieved when highway workers remove the detour signs after a major road construction project. But even as we enjoy the smooth new road, work continues: there is clean up to do. Highway workers put up new signs and remove the old ones. They pack up and cart away mobile offices. The work isn't complete until they've tidied the area. The same applies to change.

In most offices, you can find a very old technology: the bulletin board. I'm sure you, like me, have paused at one somewhere, noting items that are well past their expiration date. "Vision 2018" posters are a dead giveaway that certain items on the board need to be purged. I once found a posting asking people to prepare for a technology change that the company had implemented two years before. I helped design the poster. Embarrassing!

What happens when you see an out-of-date notice or an email signature block calling attention to a defunct project? You might chuckle to yourself or ignore it and move along. But others wonder why the team members didn't clean up after themselves. Left lying around, project artifacts can damage the credibility of the leader who didn't tie up loose ends after completing the project.

THE EVIDENCE

At the beginning of the pandemic, stores were quick to put up signs asking people to don masks and sanitize before entering. Some got creative, adding positive messages to their floor stickers reminding people to "Do your part while standing apart." Masks proliferated in an assortment of colors and designs.

As governments lifted restrictions, many artifacts of the transition were left lying around.

CLEAN UP: THE ANALYSIS

Score: C

I feel like an archeologist. I'm fascinated by the rate of decay for the symbols and artifacts left behind by the pandemic. While most stores removed pandemic signs, cleanup was not universal.

Well into the post-pandemic era, masks cluttered sewer drains and hung from rearview mirrors. Even today, some shops still have half-torn signs on their doors and heavily worn stickers on their floors. Take a walk into any mall, and you are likely to see images like the one in Figure 12.1, evidence of an era that has passed and no one wants to be reminded of, slowly being ground into the floor. They remain a blight on the appearance of stores, parks, and the banks they inhabit.

Figure 12.1 When change is adopted or the transition is over, remove the artifacts that indicated it was in progress.

LESSONS FOR CHANGE LEADERS

In the previous strategy, we looked at the importance of sustaining the behaviors we worked so hard to shift. While projects have an end date, changes should not if we want to sustain success. Change leaders must continue to reinforce desired changes in behavior to move the organization forward.

When a change needs to be extended, then all the artifacts, indicators, and guides need to be kept fresh as well, otherwise, they fade into the background with zero effect. Other than compliance reminders, leaders should remove evidence of a project once it has ended to send a clear signal that this particular change initiative has transitioned to permanence.

Take a look around. What old messages are past their prime and need to be removed in your organization? Will people come across email support addresses and web pages that are no longer valid and should be retired? Are instructions out of date? Do training courses still include material that transitions between the old and the new? Make way for the messages that matter.

TAKEAWAYS FOR YOUR CHANGE INITIATIVE

- Every change project produces artifacts: posters, memos, email addresses, training courses, and so forth.
- Refresh the artifacts that help to sustain the change.
- Remove artifacts that reflect a project that has ended.

CONCLUSION: APPLY THESE TWELVE STRATEGIES FOR SUCCESSFUL CHANGE LEADERSHIP

WHEN I VISITED JAPAN a few years ago, before the COVID-19 pandemic, I was interested to see how many people were wearing masks. Their lives were forever changed when SARS reared its ugly head. What about us? Just the other day after filling up the car with gas, I poked around in the car for sanitizer. I didn't feel clean without it. We have all been forever changed by pandemic experiences. Despite weariness from shifting guidelines and repeated lockdowns, many of us continue to carry on with certain precautions and may do so for the rest of our lives. The change has been embedded, and, from a change leadership perspective, that is success.

What have we learned about the process of leading change? Let's review the entire scope of the efforts applied by government and health leaders to alter our behavior. Here is a list of our twelve change strategies, along with each strategy's score:

Strategy	Score
Set a clear goal	A
Identify all stakeholders	B
Assess impacts	C
Develop a change plan	B
Lead the change	D
Execute the plan	A
Communicate effectively	B
Remove barriers	D
Respond to resistance	C
Measure success	B
Sustain success	A
Clean up	C

The ratings are quite a mix. We have some hits and misses, and this leads us to some important conclusions about leading change.

A HIERARCHY OF STRATEGIES

The first three strategies are the most critical: set a clear goal, identify stakeholders, and assess impacts. If the goal is not well thought out, we will head in the wrong direction. If we have a miss on stakeholders and impacts, we will target the wrong groups with the wrong messages because we will have built the wrong plan. And so on, causing a multi-car pile-up with every tactic we roll out. Every element is important to success, but they all depend on the success of those first three steps. Take the extra time to get them right. Ask tough questions to ensure you don't miss an angle.

RECOVERY IS POSSIBLE

As previously mentioned, every plan changes once execution begins. Thankfully, we can recover from a mistake, even from those first three steps. We often revisit and revise goals as we learn more. The pandemic encompassed an ongoing process of learning about the virus, symptoms, contagion, and treatments. In many respects, the deck was stacked against government and health leaders from the beginning, but these change leaders constantly course-corrected along the way.

Strong leaders do not get put off by mistakes. Perhaps one of my biggest learnings through a career of leading change is that errors, apologies, reassessment, and rededication to the goal are common. In fact, making amends often works to strengthen the commitment of those who are impacted because it illustrates that leaders are human, vulnerable, and accountable for their actions.

TURNING THE IMPACTED INTO ALLIES

If you were to ask me for one particular source for the problems in leading any change driven by disruption, I would have to call out the absence of a crystal ball. With many changes, we are aiming at a specific goal — a vision of a desirable future. But for some disruptions — like the pandemic — we remain uncertain of what the future will bring; we feel our way through it as we go. Our view of the future comes into better focus only as we progress toward it.

Why is this important? Because, as change leaders, we need to set reasonable expectations. The plan will inevitably change, yes, but sometimes even the goal will change. Leaders often pull double-duty when navigating change as they have their own challenges for embracing change while steering the ship. It's good to let your stakeholders know this.

That can be unsettling, but it also opens up an opportunity: we can engage our stakeholders as active participants in the change. Instead of being simple receivers of the change, they can be a force to help shape it. They are our eyes and ears — we need their input!

Effective change leaders build a network of trusted advisors on the front lines they can consult for honest feedback about how the change is going, whether people are really embracing it, where resistance is cropping up, how they can win over the resisters, and the overall progress toward the end goal. Remind your stakeholders that you are listening. They should feel like an important part of the change process. We can't succeed without them!

CHANGE MADE REAL

Ultimately, we return to the goal. The most important measure of success is the attainment of the target. We will never be able to truly estimate how many lives were saved from lockdowns, masks, sanitizing, and distancing, but we do know the COVID-19 virus can kill. We know it is contagious. We know sanitizing removes it, and masks can prevent us from inhaling it. So, did we reach the goal of saving lives? I'm confident we did. Did we save livelihoods? Absolutely, yes. Government cash injections kept businesses and individuals afloat.

And did people change behavior? Yes. The evidence is all around us as people now don masks to enter stores if they are fighting a cold, and parents ensure children's tiny hands are sanitized every five minutes. We see it in the continued stockpiling of rapid test kits, cleaning supplies, and toilet paper. We see it in promptly produced vaccine cards when traveling. Many of these changes are here to stay.

Leading change can be a difficult undertaking because our basic human strivings are aimed at achieving control over our own lives, and we work hard to preserve that control. It's not easy for everyone to step up when asked to do something new, different, and challenging. But we also strive to live life to the fullest, and that can motivate us to embrace change when we understand what it means for ourselves, our neighbors, our community, and our world.

GOING FORWARD: APPLYING THESE LESSONS TO YOUR CHANGE INITIATIVE

As a change leader, can you leverage the examples from the pandemic to achieve success for your own project? Yes!

I don't believe any government was directed by an expert in change. World leaders quickly applied change tactics according to what they believed would work, and — despite some severe misses — they were mostly right. As a result, we witnessed significant changes in behavior around the world. Think about what would have happened if those leaders had thoughtfully applied the strategies and tactics I've presented in this book — at the right time and at the right levels. Hmm.

Having achieved some level of adoption, governments blundered when they started firing out random tactics in desperate attempts to drive higher levels of compliance. That doesn't work. It generates resistance. Missteps and mistakes created confusion, drove resistance and even rebellion, and cost lives. While many of the positive behavior changes will endure post-pandemic, many countries will be dealing with the fallout from those blunders in terms of distrust and resistance for quite some time.

Stick to the basic strategies outlined here, and you will win over 90 percent of your audience. Unfortunately, every change project has a resistant minority. You might win them over, too, if you have the time. If not, remove them, or they will become your biggest headache and an impediment to achieving your end goal.

As a leader, you already know the basics about how to lead people through change. Give them the facts and explain what's in it for them. Aim for buy-in and avoid any sense of coercion. Make the incentive a future that's in their own best interests; tangible rewards tend to defeat the commitment we need for lasting change. Then support your people in every way possible — training, coaching, removing barriers — to demonstrate that you care about their well-being and success, not just hitting a target.

As you begin planning or refining your change project, ensure your success by following the twelve strategies presented in this book:

1. Set a clear goal
2. Identify all stakeholders
3. Assess impacts
4. Develop a change plan
5. Lead the change
6. Execute the plan
7. Communicate effectively
8. Remove barriers
9. Respond to resistance

10. Measure success
11. Sustain success
12. Clean up

So, let's get started! What would you like to change today?

If you enjoyed this book and received value, please consider leaving a review on Amazon.com.

ABOUT THE AUTHOR

ORGANIZATIONS AROUND THE WORLD struggle to implement dramatic change. That's where Jeff Skipper comes in. An expert in accelerating change, Jeff guides corporate leaders to plan and implement successful change initiatives. Leaders discover how to ignite engagement, convert grudging compliance into deep commitment, and realize their strategic goals.

Based in Canada, Jeff is an international change leadership consultant, speaker, and author of Dancing with Disruption: Leading Dramatic Change during Global Transformation. He works with organizations in energy, finance, technology, and other industries to develop the strategy that precedes effective change.

Clients, such as Bayer, BP, and The Salvation Army, have engaged him to achieve dramatic results during strategic transformation. Backed by deep expertise in leading change, Jeff guides leaders to develop effective change plans based on the twelve proven strategies he presents in his book. This empowers leaders to reach their goals faster with greater buy in throughout the entire organization.

For more than twenty-five years, beginning with a twelve-year career at IBM, Jeff has guided change projects by focusing on the people side of change. He holds a master's degree in organizational psychology and is a Certified Change Management Professional. As CEO of a transformation services company, he grew it to seven figures in just five years.

Jeff and his family live in Calgary, Alberta, Canada. When he isn't traveling, you might find him driving a Zamboni ice resurfacer at the local community arena.

To inquire about consulting and speaking, contact Jeff Skipper through www.JeffSkipperConsulting.com.

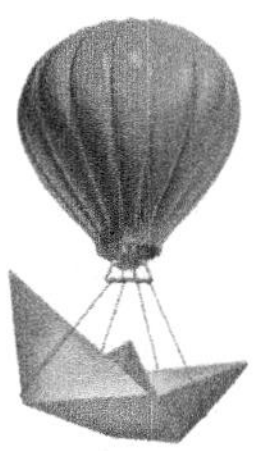

SPECIAL BONUS FOR READERS

CHANGE LEADERS – TAKE ADVANTAGE OF THESE RESOURCES

Whether you are a corporate executive or change management consultant, you'll find practical, real-world resources at Jeff Skipper's website:

- Get the best advice and strategy to lead change. Subscribe to Jeff's IMPACTED newsletter at www.JeffSkipperConsulting.com.
- For dozens of articles, videos, tools, and templates, go to Jeff's website and click the Resources tab.
- Looking to ignite engagement and accelerate the realization of your strategy? Use the two-factor "Rapid Impact Assessment" available in the Resources section.
- If you are a consultant, this is your opportunity to up-level your consulting practice: join Jeff's high-impact, strategic Change Leadership Course for Consultants. Email Jeff@JeffSkipperConsulting.com for details.

GET FREE RESOURCES AT

WWW.JEFFSKIPPERCONSULTING.COM

Made in the USA
Middletown, DE
13 May 2023

30087851R00091